The Gathering Storm

*Winds of Change in a
Post-Christian World*

The Gathering Storm

Sammy Tippit

with Dave Tippit

MOODY PRESS
CHICAGO

In memory of my mother,
Lavada Tippit,
and the influence she had on my life.

CONTENTS

PREFACE

A couple years ago I was a guest speaker at chapel service for employees of Focus on the Family; later, my wife and I had lunch with the founder and president of Focus, James Dobson. Also at our luncheon was his wife, Shirley, and Mike Huckabee, then lieutenant governor of Arkansas. As we discussed the moral state of our nation, Mrs. Dobson turned to me and asked, "Sammy, do you believe that all of these things happening today are signs that we're living in the last days?"

Her question seems to be on the minds and hearts of many others. Wherever I go, people are asking the same question: "Are we living in the last days before Christ returns?" Their question comes for good reason, as major changes are occurring in our world. As an international evangelist and traveler, I have seen changes during the past twenty-five years that I would have never imagined. I've walked into a revolution in Romania and watched the collapse of the Iron Curtain. I've been in airports not long after terrorists senselessly killed innocent people. I've watched a leading Christian musician die of the deadly human immunodeficiency virus (HIV) that produces AIDS. Fourteen years earlier it was a virtually unknown disease. I've also been in countries where bitterness passed down from generation to generation has finally yielded a brutal harvest, bringing thousands of horrendous deaths.

Meanwhile, many Western Christians sit at home, either unaware of the scope of worldwide developments or unsure how to respond to the rapid changes that are transforming our lives.

Yes, I believe the return of Christ will be soon. But even if it isn't, no one can deny the uniqueness of the times in which we live. This book is not an attempt to draw theological time lines nor choose among the pre-, mid-, or post-tribulation return of Christ. It's simply a wake-up call—a statement of urgency.

As I travel throughout the world, I've seen trends that look a lot like what I've read in the Bible about what will happen before Christ comes again. I'm not saying that what I've seen is the fulfillment of those prophecies. I'm simply saying that the stage has been set. Everything is in place for their fulfillment. The time is at hand. These are unique and challenging days.

The first two parts of *The Gathering Storm* chronicle these days. Part 1, "Thunder Among the Nations," describes how people are being corrupted by rebellions, ruthless power and killings, and deceived by false messages proclaimed by their leaders. It looks at "man's inhumanity to man." Part 2, "Rumblings from Nature," categorizes the various diseases and disasters in nature that threaten to overwhelm us as we approach the new millennium. From earthquakes and famine to various infectious diseases, they fit into the prophecies that Jesus foretold would signal the coming of end-times events.

The final part of this book, "A Beacon in the Storm," will look at the proper response to these threatening developments. The only body that can respond to the gathering storm is the church, and the only people who have hope are the followers of Jesus Christ. They must offer that same hope for the millions, indeed billions, who have little hope; the good news is God has chosen Christians to be His messengers of salvation in the gathering storm.

As Christians, how should we live in such times as these? That's the real message of this book. If you sense an urgency of the times in which we live, then read on. There's a place of safety in a storm-tossed society.

"Today is the day," and "now is the acceptable time" to know that you have a foundation upon which to stand in the midst of the storms of life. My prayer is that your life will be a bright shining light during one of the darkest moments of history.

ACKNOWLEDGMENTS

When I first began this project, I asked my son, Dave Tippit, to assist me with the research. I had no idea how much scientific and historical evidence was out there to back up my personal observations. However, Dave spent an enormous amount of time searching journals, the Internet computer network, and newspapers. The result was evidence that scientists, historians, government and law enforcement officials had come to some of the same observations as I had as I traveled the globe preaching the gospel. It would have been impossible for me to complete this book without Dave's thorough investigation of the facts.

Also, my wife, "Tex," has been very helpful in reading and rereading the manuscripts. She's offered many helpful suggestions and had many good insights. This book has, to some extent, been a family affair as Tex and Renee, our daughter, have continued to encourage me throughout the project. I appreciate their encouragement.

Also, I want to thank Jim Vincent, Julie-Allyson Ieron, and all the folks at Moody for keeping me on target with the manuscript. I appreciate working with "The Name You Can Trust," Moody Press. But I also appreciate working with people who are genuinely a part of a team that wants to impact our world for Christ.

Introduction

THE COMING
FIRE

The grass grows tall in a region of Argentina called the Pampas, so tall at times that humans can barely see one another across the grassy fields. During the heat of the summer, the grass often catches on fire. When the wind blows the fire spreads rapidly, destroying everything in its path. A visitor once asked the inhabitants of the region, "When you see the fire at a distance and the wind is blowing your direction, how do you save yourself? You know the fire will destroy everything in its path. Is there any hope for you?"

"When we see the fire at a distance, and the wind is blowing our direction, there exists only one hope for survival," one villager answered. "We start a fire in the grass immediately in front of us. As the wind blows, the fire destroys the grass before us. After the fire has completely burned the grass in front of us, we then stand on the already burned ground. When the fire from a distance arrives, it stops where the grass has already been burned, and we are saved. That's the only safe place to stand."

As we approach the close of the twentieth century and the beginning of a new millennium, signs have appeared of the impending fire storm of God's judgment. The winds of change are rapidly blowing across the pages of history, often transforming entire nations and occasionally destroying anyone or anything in their path. Many people have begun to ask, "Is there a safe place to stand during these turbulent times?" Aware that the biblical prophets foretold of judgments at the end of the world, many also ask, "What does the Bible say about these sudden changes and dramatic events that are occurring in the world today?"

The Bible has much to say about the events of human history. It clearly states that all of human history is rapidly approaching one great climax—the return of Christ to the earth. Even as Jesus came the first time, He will surely come a second time[1] In His first coming, He entered human history as a suffering servant. He came for one purpose: to die for the sins of the world. But when He comes again, He won't return as a meek and mild Savior. He'll return as the King of Kings and the Lord of Lords, coming to execute God's justice. He will bring with Him the fire of God's judgment. That will certainly be the most awesome moment of history.

THE GATHERING STORM

And preceding this monumental event will be a gathering storm that signals His return is imminent. Jesus Himself spoke of the events that would surround His return in Matthew 24. He said that when certain things begin to take place, we can know that it is summer and the season of His return is upon us. The appearing of such events implies that He will soon return with His judgment and justice. Those events include plagues, wars and rumors of wars, nation rising against nation, the acceleration of lawlessness, a global economy, a growing occurrence of earthquakes and natural disaster, and international terrorism (Matthew 24:5–14).

I am convinced that we are living in the season of His coming with the fire of God's judgment. The storm is gathering; the lightning strike will unleash the fire. In verse 33, Jesus said, "When you see all these things, you know that it

[His return] is near, right at the door." One only has to read what Jesus described as "these things" in verses 5–14 and then read the newspapers to realize that the stage is being set for Christ's return. As Parts 1 and 2 will show, such events are becoming common; Christ said that like the pain of childbirth, they would increase before He returned (verse 8).

If someone says that he has figured out when Christ shall return, you can be assured that he has been deceived. . . . No one knows that appointed time.

Can we know when His actual return will occur? Christ said, "But of that day and hour knoweth no man, no, not the angels of heaven, but my Father only" (Matthew 24:36 KJV). If someone says that he has figured out when Christ shall return, you can be assured that he has been deceived. Jesus Himself said that no one knows that appointed time. Occasionally, I hear reports of someone having made a prediction of an exact date of Christ's return. That is a complete contradiction to Christ's own words that no one knows that appointed date.

Sometimes someone will declare that his source of knowledge is an angel. The "prophet" claims to have seen an angel who revealed to him the time of Christ's return. Such reports can never be trusted because Jesus said that "not even the angels" know that appointed time when Christ shall return. Only the Father in heaven knows that day and hour.

This author is not proclaiming an exact time when Jesus will return; Christ made it clear that no one can know the exact time of His return. However, in the same passage Jesus stated, "Now learn this lesson from the fig tree: As soon as its twigs get tender and its leaves come out, you know that summer is near" (verse 32). In other words, though we cannot know the appointed time when Christ shall return, we can have a general sense that His return is imminent. Jesus listed events that would transpire immediately before He returned in Matthew 24.

Again, I am not saying that what is happening in the world today is the literal fulfillment of those passages in the Bible. But I am saying that we have entered a unique moment in history. Events transpiring in our world today have set the stage for biblical prophecy to be fulfilled. I believe that we can look upon the horizon of history and see that everything is in place for the fire of God's judgment to begin to burn. A storm is gathering, heralding the outbreak of His fire, to come with a terrible lightning strike that will set the grasses ablaze.

Powerful Changes

From twenty-five years of ministry in Eastern Europe I have learned this one lesson: When God's wind blows across history, powerful change is the norm. The entire world was shocked by the rapid collapse of the former Soviet Union; observers stood in disbelief as revelers partied among the fallen bricks of the Berlin Wall, cast to the ground. But those dramatic developments are nothing compared to what's coming—or should I say Who's coming!

Many of the events mentioned in Matthew 24, Luke 21, and much of Revelation have occurred throughout history. However, four major factors have appeared in this generation that have placed us on the fast track towards the return of Christ. They actually change the way we view such disturbances as disease and plagues, earthquakes, war, and terrorist activity. Three of the factors are new to this generation and one is as ancient as Adam's choice to disobey God in the Garden of Eden. They are transportation, communication, information, and human nature. Together they produce a uniqueness about this generation.

1. Transportation

The Germans have a quaint saying: *Die Welt ist ein kleines Dorf* ("The world is a small village"). That has never been as true as today. Air transportation has altered the course of history.

Much of it has been for good. Government officials can quickly meet face-to-face in "shuttle diplomacy" that avoids the misunderstandings of telegram or telephone communication. Gravely ill patients can be flown across country to specialized hospitals for key surgeries and treatments. Americans who once only read of the pyramids of Egypt or saw TV documentaries can now jet to the Cairo airport in less than eighteen hours and arrive at the base of the Great Pyramid of Cheops by camel the next morning. Meanwhile Britons can visit the former colony of Rhodesia, now Zimbabwe, to learn firsthand of their influence for good and bad in this growing country in southern Africa.

Air travel has even yielded spiritual benefits. Christian evangelists, pastors, and missionaries are able to bring the gospel around the world with great speed, less fatigue, and fewer physical dangers as they skirt jungle swamps and mountain peaks thanks to versatile aircraft. Moving pastors and teachers from region to region and even continent to continent is producing a greater sense of unity and identity among Christians, as well as more ways to disciple and train the worldwide body of Christ.

On January 22, 1995, I experienced one of the most incredible preaching opportunities of my entire ministry. That Sunday morning I preached at the Baptist church in the center of Khabarovsk, Siberia. It was a wonderful service. After lunch I made my way through the Siberian snow and preached at a mission of the church near the airport in Khabarovsk. I then preached that Sunday evening in suburban Seattle, Washington, at the First Baptist Church of Bothell.

Moving pastors and teachers from region to region and even continent to continent is producing a greater sense of unity and identity among Christians.

Such a thing would have been unthinkable just five years earlier. If someone would have told me in the 1980s that I would preach in Siberia on Sunday morning and in the United States the same Sunday evening, I would have thought he had seen one too many science fiction movies. But newly established commercial airline routes between the United States and Siberia (and crossing the International Date Line) now make such events realities.

International air travel has soared in the past two decades. Of the forty-seven airlines departing from Chicago O'Hare Airport, for instance, thirty-seven travel to international destinations.[2] Meanwhile, 47 million passengers crossed the North Atlantic in 1995, more than double the 23 million passengers twelve years earlier. By the year 2010 forecasters are anticipating 74.4 million passengers crossing the North Atlantic.[3] Those figures don't include Asian,

African, Australian, and South American travel to and from the United States and other parts of the world.

The increase in air travel has also had a negative impact. Terrorism is more pervasive and some would argue more effective due to the publicity and fear generated by aircraft bombings. Terrorists have used aircraft to escape for asylum, to travel to other locations to carry out terrorist acts, to hijack and threaten crew and passengers for payment of ransom or release of their comrades in terror.

Certainly terrorism is nothing new to humanity. It's as old as Cain slaying Abel. But this is a new day for terrorists, and the world has had to develop adjectives to describe terrorism. We now have "international terrorism" and "global terrorist networks." As we will see in chapter 1, the globalization of terrorism has contributed to a worldwide increase of lawlessness that the Bible predicted would happen in the last days.

Jet transportation also has been largely responsible for transmitting human and plant diseases from nation to nation and across oceans. It has been a principal carrier of virulent viruses, some of which we are still unable to cure. The most well known, of course, is the human immunodeficiency virus (HIV), which produces acquired immune deficiency syndrome, or AIDS. HIV appeared almost simultaneously on three continents during the mid-1970s. The rapid increase of HIV producing AIDS around the world has been facilitated by the ability of large groups of people to travel to any place in the world rapidly. By 1980 about 100,000 people worldwide were infected with HIV[4]. By the year 2000, at least 38 million people will be infected with HIV, according to the Global AIDS Policy Coalition, but "a more realistic projection is that figure will be higher, perhaps up to 110 million," according to the Coalition.[5] The rapid spread of the AIDS virus and its implications are detailed in chapter 5.

But AIDS is only one of numerous viruses that have begun to play havoc on nations. "Yet AIDS does not stand alone; it may well be just the first of the modern, large-scale epidemics of infectious disease. The world has become much more vulnerable to the eruption, and most critically, to the widespread and even global spread of both new and old infectious diseases," declares Jonathan M. Mann, professor of epidemiology and international health at the Harvard School of Public Health. Dr. Mann, who also directs the International AIDS Center in Cambridge, Massachusetts, attributes the new vulnerability to such diseases to our ability to move across the world.

> The new and heightened vulnerability is not mysterious. The dramatic increases in worldwide movement of people, goods, and ideas is the driving force behind the globalization of disease. For not only do people travel increasingly, but they travel more rapidly, and go to many more places than ever before.[6]

Though thousands of unknown and lethal viruses exist in the tropical and equatorial rain forests of the world, we were protected from many of those diseases in previous generations. But in the past thirty years many of those regions have been invaded by people. With the beginning of the destruction of their natural habitat, some of those viruses have proven quite adaptable. They have jumped species and left a trail of death and destruction of humanity in their path. Because of rapid mass transportation, those viruses are only twenty-four hours away from any community in the world.

The Ebola virus kills 80 percent of the people it inhabits within a couple of weeks. Waves of shock and fear spread throughout world health organizations when it reemerged the first part of 1995 in Zaire. (There will be a more thorough discussion of Ebola in chapter 4.) Had a prostitute infected an international traveler before the outbreak had been detected, the killer virus could have landed in New York, London, Tokyo, or Sydney within a matter of hours. Such a scenario would have been unlikely because of the rapid destruction that it brings with it. But it is not beyond the realm of possibility that Ebola or another deadly virus could reach any community in the world in a very short period of time.

Whether it's the globalization of disease, terrorism, or the potential of world evangelization, international transportation has set the stage for the fire of God's judgment to burn across the pages of history.

2. Communication

Communication technology has altered history in a remarkable manner. It's perhaps done more to make the world a global village than any other factor in modern civilization. Nations and masses of people have been linked together as never before in history, producing good and evil.

Consider the communications revolution in the former Soviet Union and Mongolia. One year after the Soviet Union collapsed, the doors began to open for the gospel. I had been arrested several years earlier there, but in September 1990 I stood in the stadium of the Republic of Soviet Moldavia and proclaimed the gospel to thousands of non-Christians. Soviet television filmed the first night of the evangelistic meetings and showed it throughout the Republic. I would see thousands of people throughout the former Soviet Union fill stadiums and respond to the gospel in the years that were to follow.

But even preaching on television in the former Soviet Union did not excite me as much as the plans we were making for November 1991. I met John Gibbens, head of a Bible translation effort into the Mongolian language, at the 1989 Lausanne Congress on World Evangelization.There he asked me to bring my message on prayer to the handful of believers in Mongolia. His request excited me. For two thousand years the nation had been closed to the gospel. The Buddhists rebuffed missionaries and when the communists came to power they banned all forms of religious belief and expression. But in 1990 that all changed, as Christianity entered its infant stages.

I quickly learned how limited communications were. Communication by phone was almost impossible between Mongolia and the United States. In order to coordinate the upcoming meetings Mr. Gibbens had to travel from Mongolia to Beijing, China. Only by calling from a Beijing hotel could he reach me by telephone in the United States.

After conducting Mongolia's first conference on prayer, I was invited to return for evangelistic meetings in the capital city. By the time I returned to Ulan Batar, Mongolia, just eighteen months later, communications had been upgraded significantly. In fact, I conducted a live telephone interview with a radio network in the United States from my hotel room in Mongolia. I went from not being able to communicate from the United States to Mongolia at all to being able to communicate with hundreds of thousands of people in the United States instantly from a Mongolian hotel room.

Telephones are the most pervasive form of worldwide communication. But increasingly popular personal computers and ordinary phone lines offer us the ability to communicate with university scholars and private citizens on the Internet. And satellite communication allows live reporting of world events on both radio and television.

All of these advancements in communications place the church on the verge of the fulfillment of Matthew 24:14: "And this gospel of the kingdom will be preached in the whole world as a testimony to all nations, and then the end will come." Such spiritual giants as the apostle Paul, Martin Luther, George Whitefield, John Wesley, and D. L.

Moody would have rejoiced at the opportunity to preach the gospel to the whole world. And, now, this generation stands at the threshold of the fulfillment of Christ's Great Commission.

Hate, terror, crime, and anarchy can now be communicated instantly around the world. The ideologies rooted in a lawless spirit have found the soil in which they can take root and grow.

But on the other hand, the advancements in communications technology have also opened the door for the rapid rise in lawlessness. Experts on terrorism say the technology has played into the hands of international terrorists.

Moreover, with the proliferation and sophistication of modern technology, coupled with the probability that more "have not" groups will emerge with the increase of world population, the danger of terrorism will become unbearable. At that point in time, practically all targets will be extremely vulnerable and victims of violence totally defenseless. Ultimately, then, terrorism will become more than a sporadic disruption to law and order; it will menace the very survival of civilization itself.[7]

The ultimate aim of terrorism is the overthrow of an institution or government that is perceived as the "enemy" to the terrorist organization. Terrorists are willing to utilize whatever means necessary to accomplish their objectives and have often employed fear and terror. This phenomenon is not a new one. What is new is the ability to move rapidly and communicate their dangerous ideas around the world. Eric Morris and Alan Hoe, experts on terrorism, stated in a report on international terrorism in 1987, "Money and means, transport and communication allow the modern terrorist to hit targets which previously were out of reach. . . . Modern communications, in terms of both the media and international travel, lend their support to the spread of terrorism."[8]

Hate, terror, crime, and anarchy can now be communicated instantly around the world. The ideologies rooted in a lawless spirit have found the soil in which they can take root and grow. Communications technology and international travel have allowed the lawless spirit to divide and multiply. One week after the 1995 Oklahoma City bombing of the federal building an ominous message appeared on the Internet: "I want to make bombs and kill evil Zionist people in the government. Teach me. Give me text files."[9] In 1996 police in Syracuse, New York, reported that three thirteen-year-old boys planning to blow up a local junior high school "got their bomb-making know-how off the Internet."[10]

During the ancient times God sent His judgment upon humanity because of depraved hearts and easy communication. The Scripture says, "The Lord said, 'If as one people speaking the same language they have begun to do this, then nothing they plan will be impossible for them. Come let us go down and confuse their language so they will not understand each other'" (Genesis 11:6–7). Man's heart was continually devising evil, and that darkened nature was multiplied rapidly because of his ability to communicate the evil intents of his heart. God intervened in that moment of history to prevent man from filling the world with evil.

We now stand at the same crossroads of history. We have developed networks and methods of communication that are absolutely extraordinary. That ability to communicate has produced tremendous advancements for humanity. But it also carries with it the base intents of the heart of man. It has placed humanity near the judgment of God.

3. *Information*

We live in the "information age." Computer technology has literally placed a world of knowledge at our fingertips. I enjoy Bible study on my computer. I have access to years of hard work and research. I carry my notebook computer on a plane with me and I can cross-reference passages or study the original languages of the Bible while flying to some faraway country to preach the gospel. The "information age" has certainly benefited this traveling evangelist. It's been a tremendous help to doctors, scientists, and a host of others. It's enabled intelligent, caring people to help thousands of people who would not have been helped otherwise. But there's also a down side to the "information age."

Knowledge and power without a moral base
will do nothing more than produce a greater
ability to create a temporary hell on earth.

Business executives and university students are continually told that "knowledge is power." Power can be misused, and the power available through computers is awesome. Ed Roberts, the man who created the first personal computer, said, "When you talk about power, what you're really saying is 'How many people do you control?' If I were to give you an army of 10,000 people, could you build a pyramid? A computer gives the average person, a high school freshman, the power to do things in a week that all the mathematicians who ever lived until 30 years ago couldn't do."[11] Hitler had power. So did Stalin—and a host of others throughout history. Knowledge and power without a moral base will do nothing more than produce a greater ability to create a temporary hell on earth.

Anyone from teenagers to adults can get "bomb recipes" from the Internet computer network. The first time I ventured to the Internet, I was shocked at what I found. I had never been on the "information super highway." Therefore, I wasn't too sure how to navigate. But being an adventurous soul, I wandered on the "highway" using my notebook computer. Though most was helpful and informative, I was also shocked by what I found, published in the name of "free speech." A friend aptly described it as an "electronic bathroom wall where people scribbled their dirty little thoughts." Anything from bomb making to hate speech to pornography can be found on the Net.[12]

The information age has ushered in a new era in which mankind has access to images, facts, and figures that could prove to be potentially devastating to society. Shoko Asahara, infamous Japanese cult leader, easily acquired the knowledge to produce the nerve gas sarin. He had a secret "$700,000 lab able to turn out 132 to 176 pounds a month of the nerve gas sarin—enough to kill 6 million to 8 million people."[13] In a prelude to his attack on the Tokyo subway system, 12 people were killed and 5,500 injured. Asahara was even attempting to get information on the deadly Ebola virus in order to engage in germ warfare.[14]

4. Human Nature

Those three building blocks of our modern "Tower of Babel" wouldn't be as devastating without the fourth one: human nature. Actually, all of the above building blocks have created tremendous benefits for society. They're so good that we seemingly cannot do without them. That's why we can't go back over the line and turn the hand on the clock backwards. We need those things.

The problem is that long before the ancient Tower of Babel, there was a persistent human plague called *sin*. From the time of Adam in the Garden of Eden we have struggled with a bent in our human personality towards sin. Sin is an attitude of saying "I'll do what I want to do. God or no one else can tell me what to do with my life." This attitude dwells deep in the heart of every human being. As a result we have the potential for all kinds of evil and destruction. Modern technology is only as good or bad as the people using that technology.

Science cannot offer a solution to moral problems. For instance, it might be able to produce a new vaccine for sexually transmitted diseases. But nature's viruses seem to be able to adapt and create even more devastating diseases. God created us and He knows the natural order in which mankind can live purposefully and harmoniously. He gave laws to govern our lives and enable us to live to our fullest potential. But every one of us has violated those laws. The Bible calls it sin. We all have that sin nature within us. It's that nature that produces serial murder, terrorism, divorce, perversion, and a host of other ills that are literally destroying us. When the ingredient of the fallen nature of man is mixed with instant communication, international transportation, and information technology, the result is almost inevitable: a rapid declension of moral values in society.

In the first half of this book we'll look at those biblical prophecies of what will happen before Christ returns. We'll see how these four factors have brought us to a rare moment in history—the gathering storm. It appears that summer is at hand, that only a lightning strike is needed to set a fire storm upon us. Then the fires of God's judgment will come roaring down upon humanity. The ingredients are all in place. No one knows the day or the hour when God's trumpet will sound and Christ's church will be taken up to be with Him. The fire of God's judgment will then begin to burn on earth as never before.

Part One

··

THUNDER AMONG
THE NATIONS

Through the centuries some people have chosen to follow God and others have chosen to disregard God's truth and eternal principles. But in the last few years modern transportation and communication have provided this generation with the tools to see the rampant spread of "the lawless spirit." That ability is rapidly producing spiritual and moral darkness among the nations. Civilization has found itself on the brink of disaster and moral disintegration.

A lawless spirit has arisen, as the lust for power increases and the weapons of mass destruction remain. People are pitted against people, race against race, and nation against nation. Ego-driven leaders who seem to hold no respect for God's law are rising during the chaos. The stage has been set for the "man of lawlessness" who will appear before the coming of Christ.

In the midst of the moral and spiritual vacuum, false messiahs are rapidly appearing on the scene, and the spiritually naive are following. Who would have thought that more than one hundred people from several nations would die for a self-proclaimed messiah from Waco, Texas, at the close of this century? Who would have believed that thoughtful and intelligent Japanese would follow a leader who would attempt to produce a holocaust of death and destruction in Tokyo? At the end of the twentieth century, when men and women are more educated and seemingly more civilized than earlier times, they are being duped. And despite the end of the cold war with communism, wars have neither ceased nor the threat of nuclear destruction dissipated. Thunder is rumbling among the nations of the world.

Jesus said that when these things happen, then "summer is near"—the season of His return is at hand. That season seems to be upon us. There appears to be no limit to the evil that man has devised in his heart.

There is no doubt in my mind we face a new wave of extreme Islamic radical terrorist movements. They have an infrastructure all over the world . . . .in the United States, in Europe and in Latin America.[1]

Yitzhak Rabin, April 1994
Prime Minister of Israel, who was
himself killed by a Jewish extremist in 1995

Because of the increase of wickedness, the love of most will grow cold.

Matthew 24:12

Chapter One

....

THE RISE OF THE
LAWLESS SPIRIT

Americans were stunned and outraged in 1993 when a van bomb exploded in the basement garage of the World Trade Center in New York City. The blast killed many, but its greatest toll was in the feelings of insecurity as Americans found lethal terrorism had struck on the home soil. Radical Islamic terrorists were arrested in connection with the assault.

The anger turned to fear just two years later when another bomber blew up most of the Murrah Federal Building in Oklahoma City. More than 160 people died in the blast, including several children playing in a day-care center. At first, Islamic terrorists were suspected. Then Americans felt fear and frustration as they learned that their fellow citizens were blamed for the most devastating act of terrorism in U.S. history. Fear because if a terrorist attack could take place in the heartland of America, it could happen anywhere. Frustration because it seemed such attacks cannot be prevented and anyone with a cause can use blackmail or terrorism to get attention or revenge.

Many observers wondered after the devastation in Oklahoma City, *What has happened in the world? Why are innocent men, women, and children being senselessly killed to promote an agenda of some radical group that the victims never even knew?* The arrest of anti-government militant Timothy McVeigh and an accomplice gave surface answers, but the more unsettling question remains. Why do terrorists kill, maim, and murder innocent people? How dangerous has the threat of terrorism become to the world in this generation?

I learned a little of the answer to those questions one evening a few years ago while sitting with a terrorist gang in the living room of a Northern Ireland home. I had indirectly (and unknowingly) come in contact with the terrorist group—Protestant paramilitary extremists who operated in Belfast—the first time I visited Northern Ireland a few years earlier. At the conclusion of a church service where I spoke, the pastor brought me a young lady who was weeping. I'll call her Erin. She said that she needed Christ in her heart and wanted to know God's forgiveness. I prayed with Erin, and she trusted Christ to forgive her and change her life.

He began to feel the prayers of his family and the pastor. He prayed, "God, if you want me to give my heart to You, then let me get caught before I kill this man."

Not long afterwards I received a letter from the pastor telling of the tremendous change that had taken place in Erin's life. He explained that she had been living with the leader of a Protestant terrorist organization. After giving her heart to Christ, she moved out and began to attempt to live for Christ. She asked her family to attend her baptismal service. Her parents were so impressed with the change in her life that they invited Christ to come into their lives and forgive their sins. Her brothers, who were also a part of the terrorist gang, came to the baptismal service.

At the close of the service, the pastor asked one of Erin's brothers if he wanted to place his faith in Christ. "I want to, but I can't tonight," he answered. He left knowing that he needed to open his heart and life to Christ. But he had an assignment—kill a Catholic. The pastor, the young woman, and her parents prayed that evening for him. As he drove to complete his assignment, he began to feel the prayers of his family and the pastor. He prayed, "God, if you want me to give my heart to You, then let me get caught before I kill this man."

Shortly after praying, the police stopped him and arrested him. The pastor received a phone call that evening from police headquarters. The young terrorist was broken, and he had only one request—a Bible. He gave his heart to Christ. The pastor began visiting Hugh (not his real name) in prison, helping him grow in his faith through Bible study, prayer, counsel, and books.

When I returned to Northern Ireland, the pastor told me that Hugh had read two of my books and would like to see me. I was nervous about visiting a terrorist. In the visitation room, however, I didn't meet the hard, cold individual I had anticipated but a clean-cut, handsome young man who was about the same age as my own son. When I looked into Hugh's face I could almost see my son. My heart broke. This young man would quite possibly spend the rest of his life in prison for his lawless deeds.

As we talked, it was obvious that Hugh was broken and repentant about what he had done. Now, he just wanted to share his newfound faith with others. He seemed genuine. He confessed to the police where a cache of explosives was hidden. He felt that he had to come clean with everything after his conversion to Christ. The authorities found 100,000 rounds of ammunition, hand grenades, and Sem-Tex used in explosives. Their find put his life in extreme danger. From that day on, he was a marked man. But he didn't care. He just wanted to do right with his life. He later had to be transferred to a prison where he wouldn't be killed by Protestant or Catholic terrorists. Hugh asked me to speak with his brothers, who were also a part of the Protestant paramilitary group, and his parents set up the meeting.

FACE-TO-FACE WITH A GANG OF TERRORISTS

So here I was, sitting next to several young terrorists, telling them of the conversion of their brother and former colleague in death and terror. Then I asked them about their faith. Each was either an atheist or agnostic. They had never or rarely read the Bible. They didn't have a clue about the Protestant faith of which they were supposedly defenders.

They were admittedly without God. Consequently, they were without His law which says, "Thou shalt not kill." And they certainly knew nothing of the law of God's love and forgiveness. They denied God as well as His law and became a law unto themselves.

Some experts on terrorism describe terrorist groups as often being "missionary" in nature. Often terrorists believe they have a just cause, and they want to bring it to the attention of the world. They deny the due process of law (whether it be God's law or man's law). Sometimes these groups are "religious" in nature. They often justify their actions because they are doing it "for God and His cause." Such groups may be religious, but they are certainly not Christian. They are void of God's law and eternal truth, which teaches us to "love our neighbor as ourselves" and to "forgive seventy times seven" (KJV).

This group of terrorists with whom I met displayed what the Bible describes as "a lawless spirit" that will cause "the love of most [to] grow cold" in the last days (Matthew 24:12; 2 Thessalonians 2:7–8). Jesus said in Matthew 24:12 that wickedness would increase in the days prior to His return. This increase in evil and lawlessness is included in the list of those things that Jesus mentioned in Matthew 24 which would cause us to know His return "is near, right at the door" (verse 33).

Murder, evil, and terrorism have been with mankind since Cain slew his brother near the Garden of Eden. But there's something different about what's happening today. First, those who have the lawless spirit have the capability of mass destruction as never known before. Modern technology has enabled terrorists to commit horrendous acts unknown to previous generations. The Lockerbie tragedy in which a Pan American jetliner was blown out of the sky over Scotland and the Oklahoma City bombing of a federal building merely suggest the potential destruction that's in the hands of terrorist groups.

Second, transportation has enabled modern terrorists to strike any place on earth on very short notice. Anyone can travel to any point on the globe within twenty-four hours. That creates targets for terrorists from the heartland of America to the center of London to the subway system of Tokyo, all of which have experienced terrorist attacks in the last few years. No place is now safe from those possessed with the spirit of lawlessness.

INSTABILITY AFTER THE COLD WAR

The Cold War, with its threat of nuclear attack by the Soviet Union or another communist government, came to a screeching halt with the collapse of the Soviet Union. Everyone let out a sigh of relief. We no longer needed to worry about a U.S.–Soviet nuclear holocaust.

We thought that we could now live in peace. Instead of the collapse of the Soviet Union bringing more stability to the world, it's ushered in a new era of instability. Part of that instability has been produced by economic disaster and corruption within the former Soviet Union. And part of it has been caused by terrorist vultures who have enough money to buy technology and resources from destitute Soviet agents and scientists. Now "holocaust technology" can be bought for the right price.

Louis Freeh, director of the Federal Bureau of Investigation, believes the two most serious threats to United States security are nuclear smuggling from the former Soviet Union and the explosive growth of Russian organized crime.[2] Meanwhile, the Russian mob has established a network of nuclear smuggling that could ultimately threaten civilization itself! A special report by *Newsweek* magazine concluded:

> Scariest of all is the possibility that Russia's new mobsters are piping revenues from smuggled nuclear material—all taken from the Soviet arsenal. . . . "The intercepted theft of four tons of beryllium in 1993, for example, has been linked to a bizarre conspiracy of organized crime groups in Russia and Lithuania, alleged members of the old KBG and senior government and nuclear officials," says Thomas Cochran, director of nuclear programs at the National Resources Defense Council, a nonprofit watchdog organization. There was one more conspirator: an arms merchant with a history of dealing with Middle East states and terrorist organizations.[3]

That raises some serious questions. Who's providing materials that could be used for a nuclear bomb? Who's smuggling them, and who are the buyers? What will they do with materials that could destroy entire population centers? How much is being sold on the international market? Why would anyone be willing to sell weapons of destruction to terrorists?

A key answer to the final question is, "money talks." During twenty-five years of travels to communist countries in Eastern Europe and the Soviet Union, one truth became clear: Everyone there was equal, but they were equally poor. The only way to get ahead economically was to be a part of the party system. But even that wasn't enough during the final days of communism in Eastern Europe. Everyone stood in long lines for bread and the most basic necessities.

The situation produced a system in which "the giving of gifts" became a way of survival. It was virtually impossible to exist without providing "gifts" or a "tip" to anyone in authority. Those gifts could be monetary, goods, or services. It was a way of life to the people.

Many Soviet scientists, military officials, and others found themselves unable to cope with hyperinflation. . . . Facing hunger, starvation, and destitution . . . some will sell valuable information and resources for a price.

How pervasive is this "pay-up" economy? When my daughter was hit by an automobile in Constansa, Romania, in the mid-1980s, the ambulance driver delivered her to the hospital, but couldn't enter the hospital property unless I gave the guard "a gift." I did so. In order to get on the elevator to go to the doctor's office, I had to give the elevator operator another "gift." Then, of course, I had to give the doctor a "gift" in order to speak with him. We were thankful that we had several liters of apple juice and several pounds of coffee to give away, or our daughter may not have been treated. This was simply a way of life for the Romanians and other Eastern Europeans under the domination of communism. There was no other way for survival. But that way of life left a door of terror open for the world after the collapse of communism.

When freedom came to Eastern Europe and to the Soviet Union, economic prosperity didn't automatically accompany it. Many Soviet scientists, military officials, and others found themselves unable to cope with hyperinflation, which raised the exchange rate from one dollar for one ruble before the Soviet Union dissolved to twenty-five rubles for one dollar in June 1991 (less than one year after the Soviet collapse) and five thousand rubles for one dollar four years later. The value of the Russian ruble plummeted because prices shot up extraordinarily. That meant the buying power of the average Russian citizen was virtually nonexistent.

Facing hunger, starvation, and destitution, Russians began selling whatever resources they had just to survive in the new system. Some will sell valuable information and resources for a price. According to *Time* magazine,

> Scientists earn less than $100 a month, and political control remains in the hands of the military, the KGB and former Communist Party officials. As factory subsidies erode and payrolls shrink, thousands of Russia's most talented researchers and millions of factory workers are struggling just to survive. They have thrown open the doors on a backcountry yard sale, offering all comers bargains in everything from highly sophisticated conventional-weapons systems to rare and strategic metals. . . . Foreign buyers of all sorts and sources come shopping. Some work for multinational corporations with an eye to cheap supplies. Others are front men for organized crime or outlaw regimes . . . many turn to Russians skilled in the use of *blat* (personal connections) and *vzyatki* (bribes) to oil the gears of the post empire black market.[4]

Aharon Yariv, a former head of Israeli military intelligence, said, "The former Soviet states . . . all need money, and some have military weapons and will sell them. This has to be watched. Instead of one harmful intelligence target, you have a number of easier targets."[5] Not only are there 27,000 nuclear warheads in the former Soviet Union, but it also seems that the materials to make bombs of mass destruction and the know-how may also be up for sale.[6] If a modern-day terrorist has the money, he has access to grenades, antiaircraft missiles, night scopes, and infrared sensors.

The most disturbing facet of what has transpired is that, with enough money, a terrorist group actually could buy an atomic bomb. They could hold an entire nation hostage. Before one thinks that scenario is too farfetched, keep in mind that German authorities in 1994 disclosed "that an international gang of smugglers had been peddling for $250 million nearly nine pounds of Plutonium-239 from Russia—quite possibly enough for an atomic bomb."[7]

An atomic bomb in the hands of ruthless and lawless terrorists—one can only cringe at such a thought. But this is a new day; we live on the eve of self-destruction. Leonard Spector, director of the nonproliferation project at Washington's Carnegie Endowment for International Peace, said, "We've crossed a threshold. You smuggle small amounts of the stuff often enough, and you've got a bomb."[8]

There will always be some power-hungry politician wanting to have the bomb or a money-seeking scientist willing to sell such knowledge. But with the collapse of the Soviet Union, we seem to have crossed another historical marker on the time line of human history. Weapons, technology, and resources are now capable of falling into the hands of those who have disregarded all laws of civilization in order to further their agendas. The destructive patterns and lawless deeds will be so powerful in the near future that the hearts of many will be numbed—just what Jesus said would happen right before He returns.

Weapons for Cash

But one might ask where terrorists would get the money to buy such expensive weaponry and resources. Two prime sources for cash that terrorists have turned to are rogue regimes and criminal activity, such as illegal drug trafficking. Patrick Theros, director for Regional Counter-Terrorism Affairs for the United States, spoke of how rogue regimes assist terrorists.

> With state terrorism, a country can strike at its enemies short of all-out war, and it offers terrorists numerous advantages. State support comes in many forms:
>
> - Money—terrorists spend time on operations, not robbing banks or trafficking drugs;
> - Equipment—states provide terrorists with weapons, explosives, documents, and other critical logistical support; and
> - Refuge—an important support—safe houses and sanctuary allow terrorists a respite between operations as well as time and a place to plan future actions without fear of arrest, punishment, or compromise.[9]

Theros listed seven countries that were designated by the U.S. State Department in 1994 as sponsors of terrorism: Iran, Iraq, Libya, Syria, Sudan, Cuba, and North Korea.

Terrorists also find money for their activities through drug trafficking. In 1987, Robert Landon, then president of the Association of Chiefs of Police, wrote, "*Narco-terrorism* is the term now used to describe this link between two of our most dreaded threats—terrorism and drugs. . . . In the past six or seven years, terrorist and revolutionary groups began recognizing the vast financial opportunities available in drug trafficking."[10]

Drug trafficking and terrorism are the perfect match for those who seem to possess a spirit of lawlessness. Void of the law of God, they are willing to pay any price to achieve their objectives. Life is of little value to "narco-terrorists." Donald Gregg, a former CIA station chief in Seoul, South Korea, said, "Terrorists and drug types are merciless and very hard to deal with."[11] Drug traffickers don't put their suspected informers in prison. They simply kill them.

Illegal drug trafficking is extremely lucrative, with the potential to provide terrorists with billions of dollars. *Current Health* magazine stated in 1990 that "the drug business is an ugly one, full of exploitation, wrecked health, and wasted lives. It also is a big business, the biggest in the world, with an annual volume exceeding $300 billion (some estimates go as high as $500 billion)."[12]

The collapse of the Soviet Union has provided a natural place of operation for terrorists to purchase needed resources and technology. In addition, the former Soviet republics, especially Russia, have spawned a new lawless mafia. The Russian mob is so powerful that President Boris Yeltsin referred to Russia in 1994 as a crime "superpower."[13] This new crime "superpower" has brought new links with international terrorism and international organized crime rings. And the signs are ominous.

> In this post-Cold War world gangsterdom has taken over from the Soviet nuclear and other forces as the main threat to international security. . . . Not the least concern, in this deplorable situation, is that the other nuclear superpower of the Cold War years . . . has yielded to gangs reportedly with access to some 130 tons of weapons-grade plutonium.[14]

These crime gangs have no respect for life. Vicious and deadly, when they see a business that they want, they simply take it over or force the business owners to pay protection money. A couple friends of mine were forced out of a taxi at the Moscow domestic airport and had to ride in a "mob run" taxi. The alternative could have been deadly. The mob wanted the taxi business and simply took over. The mafia has been around for a long time. But an emerging Russian mafia has the money and connections to nuclear weaponry.

One recurring, indeed primary target during all this terrorist activity is Israel. It seems logical that those with a lawless spirit would hate those to whom God gave His law. Bombings have occurred outside Israel's borders: a car bomb near a Jewish community center in Buenos Aires, Argentina, on July 18, 1994, killed ninety-six people and wounded many others. The next day a bomb killed twenty-one persons in a commuter plane in Panama. Most of the passengers were Jewish businessmen.[15] But bombings occur more frequently in Israel. In fact, during one seventeen-month period (April 1994 to August 1995) seven "suicide" bombings took seventy-three lives.[16]

Terrorist acts have a chilling effect on people's ability to love those with differing views of life. Heeding the law of love becomes difficult; hate, anger, and bitterness begin to emerge.

Every time a terrorist act is committed against innocent people in Israel it's that much more difficult for Jews to love and respect those with whom they disagree. Terrorist acts have a chilling effect on people's ability to love those with differing views of life. Heeding the law of love becomes difficult; hate, anger and bitterness begin to emerge. We can expect to see such senseless violence increase around the world as we get closer to the coming of Christ.

Jesus said "Because of the increase of wickedness, the love of most will grow cold" (Matthew 24:12). The word *lawless* is a negative form of *nomos*, the Greek word for law; thus there will be "lawlessness or wickedness."[17] Jesus said this atmosphere of no law would increase. Some translations use the words *abound* or *multiply* instead of *increase*. The Greek word is *plethuno*, which *Vine's Expository Dictionary* says in this verse literally means "shall be multiplied."[18]

Lawlessness in Place of Love

Jesus spoke of a multiplication of lawlessness that would characterize the days prior to His return. A spirit of lawlessness has always been around, but now a soil exists that lets it grow to levels previously unknown in history. Media, transportation, and historical events in the Soviet Union have produced the breeding grounds for the spirit of lawlessness to take root and multiply around the world.

The implication of Matthew 24:12 is not just how widespread this spirit of lawlessness will become, but how devastating as well. "The love of most will grow cold," Jesus warned. The words *grow cold* speak of the atmosphere that will permeate society during the last days. Vine's says the Greek verb *psucho* that is used in this verse means "to breathe, blow, cool by blowing." Thus, in the last days a wind shall blow around the world that will produce a chilling effect in the hearts of people.

Instead of love for our neighbors, fear will generally rule in the hearts of people during the last days. A person can hardly pick up a newspaper or turn on a television set today without hearing about horrible crimes being committed in his own local community. Children playing on the streets at night is no longer a safe practice. Lying in your front yard at night gazing at the stars and thinking about how big the universe must be (something I did as a child) is no longer a wise idea in most suburban neighborhoods, where security alarm systems are becoming the norm. Instead of going to sleep with the windows open and the doors unlocked, most homeowners keep everything locked tightly. It's all part of a new atmosphere that exists today, one poisoned with a spirit of fear rather than love. Lawlessness, including illegal drugs and a rise in crime, is the cause.

Terrorism has now been brought from the streets of Beirut to middle America. It's a new day, one that looks much like what Jesus described in Matthew 24. On June 5, 1995, my son, Dave, left San Antonio, Texas, to fly to Beijing, China, and on to Mongolia. He was headed there for three months of ministry. Five years earlier, my greatest concern would have been for his safety in China and Mongolia. But my greatest concern for him was that he had to fly through Los Angeles International Airport. The Unabomber had sent a letter threatening to blow up a plane in the Los Angeles airport on or around July 4. I found it somewhat strange that my greatest concern was getting my son out of America rather than into China.

What's happened? The United States isn't at war. But terrorist threats and actions have robbed the world of peace and security. As we saw in Oklahoma City, the long arm of terrorism has the potential to reach into every community in our world. The potential destruction is so great that it has begun to the chill the hearts of humanity.

The only thing worse than the rise of international terrorism in our generation would be the rise of a terrorist who thinks he is God—and has the ability to convince others that he is God. Before you think that could never happen to educated people in this era, read on.

... but a century of wars, natural disasters and political extremism has produced spiritual confusion. Out of this have emerged those self-elected gods and followers who not only destroy themselves but insist on taking others with them.[1]

Ian Buruma
Correspondent, *Time* magazine

. . . .

Jesus answered: "Watch out that no one deceives you. For many will come in my name, claiming, 'I am the Christ,' and will deceive many. . . . For false Christs and false prophets will appear and perform great signs and miracles to deceive even the elect— if that were possible. See, I have told you ahead of time."

Matthew 24:4-5, 24-25

Chapter Two

....

FALSE MESSIAHS
AND FALSE PROPHETS

The temperature had warmed to minus 50 degrees Fahrenheit this January day in a remote region of Siberia. I had come to preach the gospel, but I wondered whether people would come to our meetings in such severe weather conditions. What would the spiritual temperature be in such a remote region of the world?

I quickly learned that the spiritual temperature was warm indeed. Everywhere we traveled, people were seeking answers to spiritual questions. Sometimes, though, there was spiritual confusion as well. One evening before beginning the meeting in a sports arena, I received an envelope from a middle-aged woman.

"Mr. Tippit, excuse me, but could I speak with you?" she asked in very good English. "I wanted to tell you that I have met Christ."

I smiled, thinking that she was speaking about her conversion experience. "That's wonderful," I said. "When did you come to know the Lord?"

"Last summer. And I have a picture of him that I would like to give you." She then pulled out a picture of a man with long flowing brown hair who looked very similar to pictures one might see of Jesus in Christian bookstores. "He lives here in Siberia and he's wonderful. He's the messiah. There are thousands of us who have come to know him, love him, and follow him. I thought that you also might want to meet him."

As I tried to regain my composure, I said, "You seem to be a very intelligent woman. You need to know that Jesus said in the last days there would be many who would rise up and say, 'I am the Christ.' I can assure you that this man is not the Christ. He is simply a fulfillment of the prophetic words of Jesus when He described world conditions in the last days." Her face dropped as disappointment set in. I explained more about false messiahs and encouraged her to listen closely to my message on the second coming of Christ. She did and responded during the invitation time to follow Christ. A local pastor counseled her and began to minister to her. Yet thousands of others have followed that self-proclaimed messiah.

Their response has amazed me, as many areas have not heard the gospel until recently. I've stood in stadiums and public arenas in the most remote regions of Russia, where the gospel had not been previously proclaimed publicly. In every remote city or village I have visited, the same situation exists: a strong base of spiritism has developed, causing people to be very open to cults and occult groups.

THE APPEAL OF FALSE MESSIAHS

The rapid rise of cults in the former Soviet Union has amazed me. Many people have entered cultic practices in the former Soviet Union, a land where communists had systematically brainwashed the citizenry with atheism from preschool to postgraduate university training. But the trend isn't accelerating only in the former Soviet Union. There seems to be a rapid rise of self-proclaimed messiahs and false prophets gathering followers at an alarming rate around the world. J. Gordon Melton, author of *Encyclopedia Handbook of Cults in America,* estimates that at least seven hundred cults are active in the United States.[2] False messiahs and false prophets have popped up in Eastern Europe, Western Europe, Asia, and North America during the 1990s. They have wooed people with promises of peace, prosperity, and a new world order. Often they have claimed God's sanction for their mission, as they espoused a philosophy of love and personal sacrifice. In some instances they have left behind a trail of disappointment; in other cases death and destruction have followed them.

False messiahs and false prophets . . . are rising on every continent with an unusual ability to gather followers, many of whom are willing to die or even kill for their messiah.

Jesus told His disciples in Matthew 24, "when you see all these things, you know that it [His return] is near, right at the door" (verse 33). Included in Jesus' list of "these things" is the rise of false messiahs and false prophets. This seems to be such an important item in the list that Jesus states it twice. The first time He mentions it is a direct response to His disciples when they asked, "When will this happen, and what will be the sign of your coming and the end of the age?" (verse 3). He warned them not to be deceived and said that many would make the claim, "I am the Christ." He then reiterated His prophecy and warning in verses 23—25, saying, "False Christs and false prophets will appear and perform great signs and miracles to deceive even the elect—if that were possible."

False Messiahs at the End of the Millennium

False messiahs and false prophets have been around

51

for a long time. However, in the final decade of this millennium there seems to be a rash of false messiahs and false prophets. They are rising on every continent with an unusual ability to gather followers, many of whom are willing to die or even kill for their messiah. Mass media contribute to their popularity, publicizing their teachings and helping these false messiahs gain a stronghold in the hearts of people.

From David Koresh in Waco, Texas, to Shoko Asahara in Tokyo, Japan, followers of these new messiahs have been arming themselves for one last apocalyptic battle. The deception of some self-proclaimed messiahs has motivated their followers to commit suicide and even acts of terrorism for their leader. Asahara's sect was blamed for releasing the deadly sarin gas in Tokyo's subway, killing several people and wounding more than five thousand.

Experts on terrorism have become very concerned about the present trend. *Time* magazine reported in 1995 that, "The events in Tokyo were a clear warning to the world. Terrorism has taken a step across a threshold that security experts have been anticipating with dread for decades. It has been known that there are groups out there that are willing to kill at random."[3] Robert Kupperman, a terrorism expert at the Center for Strategic and International Studies, commented further, "Nightmares are coming true. I think we're in for deep trouble."[4]

Experts are observing exactly what Jesus said would occur immediately before His return. Mere men who make themselves out to be gods and have the ability to convince others of the same, could produce an era of terror, fear, and chaos unknown in history. These new messiahs now have modern technology available to them that could cause havoc in the most advanced and sophisticated societies. Consider the following false messiahs of the 1990s and their use of technology and charisma to manipulate and terrorize people.

Waco, Texas, USA; 1993

The first major report of a false messiah in the 1990s occurred in America's own backyard. In the sleepy central Texas town of Waco, journalists from around the world converged to cover a siege at the compound of the Branch Davidians, an end-times cult. Their leader, David Koresh, reportedly had told his followers, "If the Bible is true, then I'm Christ."[5] More than one hundred ATF (Alcohol, Tobacco, and Firearms) federal agents had gone to the compound to arrest Koresh for stockpiling weapons and other offenses. He and his followers determined to wait out a siege with the government, and one hour after the attempted arrest, four agents were dead and sixteen wounded, and ten followers of Koresh reportedly had been killed.

Koresh and his followers had prepared themselves for a great battle. The compound just outside of Waco was more of a military fortress than a house of worship. The Davidians held out for fifty-one days. In the end most of the people inside—ninety-one men, women, and children—died as the compound burned to the ground.

Network television carried the scene live into the homes of stunned Americans, and questions about the ATF and FBI assault on the compound would linger with Americans for months to come. But the question that seemed to have no answer was *why?* Why did the tragedy have to happen? Why would men, women, and children follow a high-school dropout all the way to their death?

Koresh, whose birth name was Vernon Howell, was expelled from the Seventh-day Adventist Church in 1984. According to *Time* magazine, "In 1990 he changed his name legally to Koresh, Hebrew for Cyrus, the Persian king who allowed the Jews to return to Israel after their captivity in Babylon. His apocalyptic theology converged with secular survivalism, with its programs for hunkering down amid stockpiles of food and ammo to endure a nuclear holocaust or social collapse."[6]

A false messiah had emerged right in the middle of the Bible Belt of America. He was able to attract followers from Britain and Australia as well as the United States. Some of the men were so convinced of his deity that they would be willing to give their wives and children to Koresh for his sexual pleasures. Marc Breault, a member of the Davidian cult in 1988 and 1989, said, "He [Koresh] was fixated with sex and with a taste for younger girls. He began to teach that all the women in the world belonged to him and only he had the right to procreate." Another former member of the cult explained that Koresh taught that, "God believed it was necessary to send him down to be a sinful Jesus so that, when he stood in judgment of sinners on Judgment Day, he would have experience of all sin and degradation."[7]

Many of us have a difficult time understanding how anyone could believe such irrational and immoral teachings. We must remember that Jesus said, "Watch out that no one deceives you. For many will come in my name, claiming, 'I am the Christ,' and will deceive many" (Matthew 24:4–5).

Kiev, Ukraine; 1993

After the collapse of the Soviet Union, the White Brotherhood cult quickly gained in popularity, soon drawing an estimated 500,000 followers from throughout the former Union.[8] A Russian engineer, Yuri Krivonogov, founded the cult shortly after the fall of communism. He became the chief prophet, telling of the coming judgment and proclaiming his wife, Marina Tsvygun, the cult's messiah. Like Koresh, Marina changed her name. Her new identity became Marina Devi Khristos. Krivonogov became a false prophet gathering a following and then proclaiming his wife the messiah. Amazingly, hundreds of thousands of people followed Marina. Jesus warned of such false prophets and messiahs in the last days.

Posters with Marina's picture were placed in Moscow, Kiev, and other population centers in the former Soviet Union. Under her picture was written, "I am the living god and through me alone can you receive redemption against Judgment Day."[9] When she was arrested in Kiev, authorities feared a mass suicide. Marina, who had been a former communist leader, told authorities, "I am Maria Devi Khristos. You are all servants of Satan and the devil." And referring to the death of Jesus, she said, "Just like [He was] 2000 years ago, I am thirty-three years old."

Then there's the Siberian cult leader whom I mentioned at the beginning of this chapter. Thousands are following him. Thus far he hasn't proven to be physically harmful to society. But he is another tragic example of the uniqueness of the times—a generation in which false messiahs seem to be multiplying.

Granges-Sur-Salvan, Switzerland; 1994

Luc Jouret, much like David Koresh, was consumed with thoughts of stockpiling weapons for one last, great battle. "In 1993 he fled Canada after pleading guilty to charges that he had tried illegally to obtain three guns with silencers."[10] In Switzerland he started the Solar Temple Cult and found approximately two hundred people and another seventy-five in Canada who would follow him. This messianic figure was able to convince or coerce his followers to die with him and for him.

In October 1994 forty-eight members of the cult died a horrible death as chalets in two Swiss villages, Cheiry and Salvan, burned to the ground. Members of the cult had either committed suicide or had been murdered. Several were found with bullet holes in the head. Others had written suicide notes. Another five cult members were found dead with stab wounds in Canada. In Cheiry, firemen searching through the rubble found champagne bottles scattered around the floor, indicating a morbid final celebration before the mass suicides and murder. The bodies were found "in a circle with their faces looking up at a portrait of a Christlike figure resembling Jouret."[11]

Tokyo, Japan; 1995

Shoko Asahara is perhaps the most notable of the false messiahs by the midpoint of the 1990s. He founded and became the messianic leader of the Aum Shinrikyo (Aum Supreme Truth) cult. The cult claimed to have 10,000 followers in Japan and well over 30,000 in other countries. Asahara was able to attract thousands of spiritually starved Japanese and Russians, many of them highly educated. Included were lawyers, scientists, computer experts, and other professionals. He spoke in Moscow to 15,000 people and claimed close to 30,000 followers in Russia. According to press reports Asahara's cult had been paying $800,000 a year to broadcast a daily, prime-time program on Moscow's Mayak radio station and had a weekly television broadcast on Moscow television.[12]

This Japanese messiah admired Adolph Hitler and predicted the end of the world in the nineties—as early as 1997. In one of his books, Asahara wrote, "I hereby declare myself to be God."[13] He not only had the charisma to convince some of Japan's brightest and best of his deity, but he was also able to persuade them that the world would soon come to an end. In his scenario, the United States would launch a nuclear attack on Japan. Only 10 percent of the population plus his followers would survive.[14]

He not only believed in this great battle, but he is accused of attempting to initiate a great catastrophic event that would hasten the day of Japan's fall with a nerve gas attack in Tokyo. The assault on the subway of Tokyo was a terribly frightening tragedy for the Japanese people. One photographer described the scene, "I saw several dozen people on the platform who had either collapsed or were on their knees unable to stand up. One man was thrashing around on the floor like a fish out of water."[15]

> *The cults have thrived in surroundings of secularism and materialism, two philosophies that dominate the 1990s.*

Sarin gas carries memories of Hitler's attempt to exterminate the Jews during World War II. It brings shivers to the hearts of everyone who hoped that such atrocities would never again be committed in human history. But police had plenty of reasons to suspect that the followers of Asahara had the potential to create another holocaust as this millennium comes to a close. Close to one thousand police raided the headquarters of Asahara's cult just weeks after the March 1995 attack.

Day after day they [police] emerged with ton after ton of chemicals—sodium cyanide, sodium flouride, phosphorous trichloride, isopropyl alcohol, acetonitrile—some benign, but others deadly, and still others that if mixed together might create something deadlier still. Enough to kill 4.2 million people, guessed one newspaper; another topped it with an estimate of 10 million.[16]

Why Now?

One can't help but wonder why people follow such

obviously false messiahs in an age of secularism. Undoubtedly, there's been extremely rapid growth among cults in the last several years. But, why? This is the age of scientific reason, a time when it appears trendy to attack faith in God.

One factor links the four self-proclaimed messiahs and their followers. The cults have thrived in surroundings of secularism and materialism, two philosophies that dominate the 1990s. When life is defined only in terms of material, then society will begin to produce weird aberrations of faith. People, created in the image of God, have a natural and deep longing to know the God who created them. When that longing is suppressed by society, it will always result in aberrations of genuine faith. This hunger for God can be so intense that people will do anything or follow anyone who says that they know the way to God.

Of course, the former Soviet Union had dictated for seventy years that mankind and life in general was only material. The official philosophy of the state was dialectical materialism. But the West hasn't been far behind in promoting a philosophy rooted in a belief in materialism. Capitalistic materialism will leave Western society just as empty as dialectical materialism left Eastern Europe. In fact, while I have preached in schools throughout the former Soviet Union since the collapse of Communism, I would never be allowed to mention the name of Christ in most public schools in America today.

The United States, Japan, Switzerland, and Canada would be at the top of the world's list of prosperous societies. And it's in those countries that cults seem to flourish. It's those nations where materialism has left a great void in the hearts of their citizens—one so large that some of their people would even kill or die for self indulgent egomaniacs who say they are the Christ. Materialism, in any form, will only intensify and distort man's hunger for God.

The most obvious examples of this thirst for God can be found in the former Iron Curtain countries. Many people who have traveled to Eastern Europe are shocked at the intense spiritual hunger in the former Soviet Union and Eastern European countries since the collapse of the Iron Curtain. But it's really nothing new. In 1973 two friends and I infiltrated the Communist Youth World Festival in East Berlin, a gathering of 100,000 committed young communists from around the world, in order to share our faith in Christ. We were pleasantly surprised to see two hundred of those hard-core Communist young people decide to turn from their sin and put their faith in Jesus. After that fest I began traveling throughout Eastern Europe and found an intense hunger for God.

In 1980 I entered Romania for the first time. The hunger for God was unlike anything that I had seen anywhere. Interestingly, Romania was one of the most repressive regimes against Christians. But everywhere I traveled churches were full and overflowing. People on many occasions stood in the streets to hear the gospel of Christ. There was somewhat of a mathematical formula that became clear in my mind:

Suppression of Faith = Intense Hunger For God
Greater Suppression of Faith = Greater Hunger For God

I entered Romania again on January 1, 1990, during the revolution, one week following the death of the evil dictator, Nicolae Ceaucescu. I witnessed something that I believe clearly illustrates today's situation in Eastern Europe. The Romanian flag was flying everywhere. It was draped out of apartment buildings, offices, and government headquarters. But all of the flags had a hole in the middle of them. The Romanians had cut a hole in the center of the flag, removing the symbol of communism. The masses had been taught the philosophy of dialectical materialism—and it had failed them. They detested the old philosophy.

Meanwhile, thousands of people took to the streets in population centers throughout the nation. They would spontaneously shout, *"Exista Dumnezeu! Exista Dumnezeu!"* which translated means, "There is a God! There is a God!" Faith erupted like a gusher in the hearts of the people.

With such openness of hearts, cults began to flood into Eastern Europe. There were not only the cults of false messiahs. The well-plowed soil of seventy years of secularism had produced fertile ground for all sorts of religious groups to pour into those nations. Many of them were nothing at all like the deadly "messiah" cults. They were peaceful and physically harmless. However, their teachings were completely contrary to biblical Christianity. Groups such as Jehovah's Witnesses and Mormons have made a major impact in Eastern Europe. And yet their teachings run contrary to the great historic and biblical doctrines of the Christian faith. Hare Krishna dancers and singers could be found regularly on Moscow streets near Red Square.

I've traveled to some of the most remote regions of the former Soviet Union. Everywhere I've gone, I've found tremendous spiritual hunger. However, hunger without repentance and a biblical understanding of God opens the heart to all kinds of false teaching from would-be prophets and messiahs. It seems as the twentieth century comes to a close, people are desperately looking for someone to guide them spiritually—anyone with any belief system. Their search opened the door for false prophets and messiahs on almost every continent to deceive thousands.

Jesus said that in the last days before His return "false Christs and prophets would appear and perform great signs and miracles to deceive even the elect, if that were possible." As the millennium closes, prophecy unfolds before our very eyes as we watch Satan make an all-out attempt to manipulate and deceive the heart of man.

The Cold War has been replaced by small but numerous fires all over the world: Afghanistan, Angola, Burundi, Haiti, Iraq-Kuwait, Liberia, Rwanda, Somalia, Western Sahara, and the former Yugoslavia—not to mention the conflicts that have arisen in the former USSR since the demise of Pax Sovietica or the problems that are still simmering in Cambodia, Cyprus, El Salvador, the Middle East, Mozambique and elsewhere.

The nature of the strife has also changed: Interstate wars have been largely replaced by violent conflicts within states, many of them legacies of divisions fostered during the Cold War and even back to colonial times.[1]

Ruben Mendez
Historian for the United Nations
Development Program

....

You will hear of wars and rumors of wars, but see to it that you are not alarmed. Such things must happen, but the end is still to come. Nation will rise against nation, and kingdom against kingdom. . . . Wherever there is a carcass, there the vultures will gather.

Matthew 24:6, 7a, 28

Chapter Three

....

WARS AND
RUMORS OF WARS

Jesus listed in Matthew 24 those historical events that must transpire before He returns. One of the most horrifying developments included in that list is war. Before He comes again, the instances as well as the devastating effects of war will increase. In its savagery and pain, war thunders words of hatred among peoples and nations.

Let's not forget that war is unnatural. Man was created to live and love, not to kill and hate. But in the last days, Jesus prophesied, hatred and bitterness among nations and groups of people will run at an unprecedented high. There will be so much war that it will be hard to keep up with all the places where it has broken out. Jesus said there will be "wars and rumors of war."

Later in Matthew 24 Jesus described the conditions of the times prior to His return. The devastation would be so bad that vultures would be feeding off the dead bodies that are lying in the open (verse 28).

Such devastation is hard to conceive. As a post-World War II "baby boomer," I wasn't drafted to fight in the Vietnam War, but many of my peers and friends were. I watched them return home changed. Some tried to escape what they had seen and experienced by popping pills, smoking marijuana, or drowning themselves in alcohol. It was hard for me to understand what they were feeling, until the fall of 1995 when I traveled to Rwanda. Death and destruction were so horrible in the country that it's still difficult for me to talk about what I saw and heard. I never imagined that people could be so greedy, bitter, and fearful that they would do the things that were done in the name of war.

The militia used guns, hand grenades, and even machetes to kill Tutsis. And loyal Hutus even killed their neighbors, tossing bodies in the river. In fact, many bodies thrown into the river floated down to Lake Victoria. At the height of the atrocities, Ugandans reported finding up to one thousand bodies per day that had washed up on the shores of Lake Victoria. In one church compound five thousand people were butchered. The skeletons, clothes, and church items were still lying there. Nothing had been removed. The church had turned into a house of horrors.

The killings came after the president's own military, angered at their leader's willingness to negotiate with the majority Tutsi tribe, shot down his plane. Like the president, the military were part of the Hutu tribe, and they had brought their people to power in 1960. The Hutu government had allowed almost two million Tutsis to remain in Rwanda, and those Tutsis had integrated peacefully into the life of the nation. But those who fled the country weren't allowed to return. After negotiations failed to reconcile the two groups, an offensive against the nation was launched by Tutsis living in Uganda. Guerrilla warfare and skirmishes continued from the early 1990s until April 1994.

The Hutu president himself had preached a message of hatred for the Tutsis during his reign. Now with their leader dead, the military ordered the extermination of all Tutsis living in the country. Holocaust broke out. The distrust and hatred between the country's two largest ethnic groups—and members of two ancient kingdoms—the Hutus and Tutsis, had spanned generations. Now it spilled out in savage killing, and fearful Tutsis fled for their lives.

When I returned from Rwanda, the leader of a Bible study at my church asked me to recount my experiences for those in class. As I stood to speak, I broke down and wept. To describe what I had seen and heard seemed impossible, for the scenes were overwhelming. Before I left, one Rwandan friend said to me, "Sammy, our hearts are very sick and we desperately need healing." I had tasted of their sickness.

The 1994 genocide in Rwanda stands as one of the great atrocities of this century. Press reports said that 500,000 people were killed in one month during the genocide. But every Rwandan we met said that the figure was more than one million people slaughtered. The genocide was so bad that the United Nations' 1,700-member peace-keeping force was withdrawn. Belgian peacekeepers reportedly were so frustrated at what they had seen that they burned their blue UN berets before boarding their flight.[2]

NATION AGAINST NATION

The Rwanda holocaust is not the first attempt at genocide; the Nazi holocaust remains an indelible black mark on the twentieth century. But it does fit Jesus' prophecy that "nation will rise against nation and kingdom against kingdom." The brutal fighting among Serbians, Bosnians, and Croatians in the former Yugoslavia, now four independent countries, is another instance of nation opposing nation. The Serbian military engaged in "ethnic cleansing," a euphemism for genocidal killing, and reports during and after the war in Bosnia described brutal mass executions and deportations of village residents. Angry Bosnians have retaliated with brutalities of their own.

A look at warfare in three regions of the world illustrates how fighting among nations, rather than abating at the end of the Cold War, has merely changed into "numerous fires all over the world,"[3] according to UN historian Ruben Mendez.

THE WAR IN RWANDA

I entered Rwanda only one year after the holocaust at the request of evangelical church leaders. As I talked with the leaders and other people and observed the evidence, I soon realized that the atrocities in this country were different in kind from those committed against the Jews by the Nazis during World War II. The Nazis attempted to cleanse their culture of Jews just as the Hutu military tried to kill all of the Tutsis, yet there was one primary difference. In Nazi Germany, Jews were sent to concentration camps and slaughtered by evil, elite Nazi henchmen. But in Rwanda much of the population participated in the slaughter of innocent men, women, and children.

I'll never forget my meeting with the present mayor of Butare, Samuel Gasana. He is a Tutsi. Before the holocaust he worked at the library of the National University of Rwanda in Butare. What happened to his family illustrates how widespread and evil the hatred was. And his story wasn't the worst that I heard.

When the order was given to kill all Tutsis, utter chaos broke out. People didn't know what to do. Tutsis living in the country tried to find places of safety. They turned to anyone that they thought they could trust.

In the case of Samuel Gasana, the future mayor of Butare and his family sought refuge in the homes of trusted friends and fellow professors at the university. Because his family is large, one of his trusted friends told him, "You'll never be able to be hide your seven children, your wife and yourself in one place. I'll hide five of the children and you can find another place for your wife, two children, and yourself." The mayor agreed. But as soon as the "trusted friend" had the children in his home, he called for the militia. They came and slaughtered the children.

Some Hutu women married to Tutsi men had their husbands killed, and some Hutu men slaughtered their own wives. Some parents of mixed marriages even killed the children who had physical features of the Tutsi parent. So many people were killed that it has taken over a year to bury all the dead. When we arrived a year after the atrocities, they were still trying to bury the dead in mass graves.

There were so many people killed during the attempted genocide that bodies were littered all over the highways. It was exactly as Jesus described, when he spoke of the devastation of the last days where vultures would gather to feast upon the carcasses. In Rwanda, the dogs fed upon the carcasses of many dead people scattered across the countryside. Consequently, the soldiers were ordered to shoot and kill the dogs.

THE WAR IN BOSNIA

In the ethnic conflict between the Serbians, Bosnians, and Croatians in the former Yugoslavia, their weapons have been more sophisticated than those of the Rwandans. Hatred and ethnic conflict there is rooted in years of bitterness between ancient kingdoms. I visited Yugoslavia immediately prior to its dissolution to conduct a pastors and Christian leaders conference. Upon deboarding at the Belgrade airport, I went to a car rental agency for my vehicle. The man at the counter asked me what kind of news reports I had heard about the problems between the Serbians and Croatians. Because I didn't know the man, I tried to be evasive in my response.

"I am Serbian," he responded. "I have many Croatian friends. Some were in my wedding party. But I would kill them in a minute!"

I was stunned. "Why?" I asked. "Why would you even say such a thing?"

The man was obviously younger than I, but he began to talk about World War II and how the Croatians had sided with Hitler. "You weren't even alive during World War II," I responded. "Why would you want to kill your friends over something that took place when both of you weren't yet alive?" He didn't have an answer.

At the close of this century, such age-old hatreds and feelings of bitterness between ancient kingdoms and peoples are rising to the surface. In visiting several war zones through the years, one lesson stands out: Bitterness and hatred held in the human heart doesn't just affect the person harboring those feelings. Those destructive feelings can be passed down to the children for generations to come and produce chaos and devastation in their lives.

That makes this generation one that's more vulnerable than any other time in history. These ancient animosities have been around for a long time. But there's never been the weaponry with which such devastation could be inflicted on entire populations as the weapons we have today.

The hatred in Bosnia-Herzegovina and the surrounding former Yugoslavia republics traces back to the murder of Archduke Franz Ferdinand by a Serbian terrorist in the Bosnian town of Sarajevo. Ferdinand's assassination was rooted in some of these ancient disputes among different kingdoms of people in the Balkans; his death sparked World War I. Eighty years later, many of those old hatreds are resurfacing today. If World War III were to erupt from those conflicts, the kind of destruction and toll on mankind would be absolutely unthinkable. We have weapons of mass destruction today that could produce the kind of horror that civilization has never known.

Civilization may already be flirting with such a disaster. My son, Dave, was in Siberia during the summer of 1995. When I telephoned him during August, he asked about the

Serbian-Bosnian conflict. He was concerned because the Russian media were reporting that World War III was possibly about to begin. Of course, the Russian media were wrong. But it's difficult for many Westerners to understand Eastern Europe's concern about tensions in the Balkans. Conflict in the region has already sparked one world war, and some military analysts believe that those age-old tensions could ignite another worldwide military conflict.

WARS AND POTENTIAL WARS IN THE BALKANS

The Serbians, Croatians, and Bosnians have fought the last several years over territorial disputes. Yet, their disagreements aren't the only ones in the Balkans. Austin Bay, an author who writes extensively about military and intelligence issues, listed tensions and potential places of battle in the Balkans:

Bulgaria. Has latent claims on parts of Grecian Thrace, Turkish Thrace, Grecian Macedonia, claims part of the southern Romanian coast.

Greece. Claims parts of southern Albania; has latent claims to Macedonia; covets Turkish Thrace; claims numerous parts of Turkey outside of the Balkans.

Romania. Claims slices of Serbia's border area; claims the whole nation of Moldova (a former republic of the Soviet Union).

Albania. Claims Kosovo Province and parts of Montenegro. Albanian nationalists in western Macedonia are beginning to clamor for unification with Albania.

Hungary. Some right-wing groups in Hungary claim Transylvania (now in Romania). Hungarian ultranationalists also claim Serbia's Vojvodina region.

Serbia. In addition to claiming Serb-dominated portions of Bosnia and Croatia, some Serb ultranationalists claim the Republic of Macedonia.

Slovenia. Some Slovenes claim the Italian port of Trieste.

Croatia. Croatian ultranationalists claim the whole of Bosnia. And the Slovenes are wrong—Trieste belongs to Croatia.

Italy. Italy has latent claims to the Dalmatian (Croatian Adriatic) coast.

Republic of Macedonia. Some Macedonians claim parts of Greece, Bulgaria, Serbia, and Albania—i.e., the countries that claim Macedonia. (Currently, 1500 U.S. soldiers patrol the Serbo-Macedonian border.)

The Balkans are an explosive Mosaic. [4]

I have visited many of those countries: Romania, Moldova, Albania, Hungary, Serbia, Croatia, Macedonia, and Greece. I can attest to the fact that the region is a potential powder keg. Significantly, however, the tension was largely dormant until the breakup of the Soviet Union and the collapse of communism in Eastern Europe. When communist Yugoslavia dissolved, the door swung open for the Serbian-Bosnian-Croatian war. Dictatorial communism had controlled the people, leaving those tensions no avenue of expression.

Does this mean that only a tightfisted dictator will be able to bring renewed stability to the region? Perhaps. While I do not espouse such a development, it could occur. And that has other implications for fulfilled biblical prophecy—a dictatorial world leader who offers a plan for peace.

A NEW TRIBALISM AND A NEW WEAPONRY

Tensions between groups of people seem to be running at an all-time high. North Americans and Western Europeans are angry about the new wave of immigrants flooding into their countries. In 1995 separatists in Quebec led a nearly successful campaign to make the mainly French-speaking province independent of Canada; another election on the issue is expected. In Scotland, nationalists wish their country to declare independence from the United Kingdom of Britain. In the United States, racial tensions continue.

Once the decision was made by the United States to produce and deploy the atomic bomb at the end of World War II, the world could never again be the same.

In addition, a new global class struggle appears to be emerging, pitting the haves in technology and prosperity with the have-nots. Worldwide economic conditions seem to be fostering a spirit of bitterness and anger among people. Ray Marshall, former U.S. Secretary of Labor under President Carter, wrote in the fall of 1995,

> The world is experiencing the worst employment crisis since the 1930s. Almost one-third of the earth's 2.8 billion workers are either jobless or underemployed, and many of those who are employed work for very low wages with little prospect for advancement. [5]

Whether it be racial, economic, technological, ethnic, or national divisions, the world is headed on the course of historical events that Jesus predicted would take place before He returned. A new kind of tribalism is emerging around the world as nation rises against nation, kingdom against kingdom, race against race, and economic class against economic class.

But what really makes this course so dangerous is the weaponry presently in the hands of modern civilization and our ability to deliver those weapons anywhere. Once the decision was made by the United States to produce and deploy the atomic bomb at the end of World War II, the world could never again be the same. There will always be some power-hungry dictator willing to pay for the knowledge and use of modern weapons of destruction. And there will be some money-hungry businessmen and scientists willing to deliver the necessary information and materials. The aspirations of Saddam Hussein in the Gulf War has vividly taught us this lesson. When Major General Hussein Kamel al-Majid, the former head of Iraq's clandestine weapons programs, defected in August 1995, he brought with him confirmation of Iraq's biological, chemical, and nuclear capabilities.[6]

Madeline Albright, United States ambassador to the United Nations, gave the U.S. Congress startling details of Iraq's biological weapons systems. She reminded congressmen that Iraq had admitted to having produced deadly anthrax and botulism toxin, adding:

> Although limitations on delivery capability would limit potency, it is at least theoretically true that the amount of biological warfare agents Iraq admitted producing is more than enough to kill every man, woman and child on Earth. We believe that the Iraqis began their biological warfare program much earlier than they have admitted, and that more biological agents were manufactured and many more facilities and people involved than Iraq has revealed.[7]

Newsweek noted: "Since the stunning revelation [in August 1995] that Iraq had manufactured tons of biological weapons before the Persian Gulf War, new evidence has emerged of a program more extensive, and potentially more lethal, than outsiders imagined. The Iraqis turned a broad array of bacteria and viruses into tools of offensive warfare."[8] Reporter Christopher Dickey described three of the biological weapons: a virus that blinds its victims, a pustular disease called camel pox that can be fatal, and "a germ that causes shrapnel wounds to develop gas gangrene . . . that produces balloonlike sores on the skin" and also can be fatal.[9]

Press reports also indicated that Iraq was well on the way to developing atomic and chemical weapons of mass destruction as well.[10] Similarly, North Korea has nuclear, chemical, and biological capabilities. "By the mid to late 1990s the DPRK [Democratic Peoples Republic of Korea] would have perfected the nuclear-tipped NoDang-X ICBM that is capable of reaching the continental U.S.," reports Yossef Bodansky, director of a congressional task force on terrorism and unconventional warfare. "This fact alone will introduce a whole new dimension to the crisis in Korea."[11]

One of Bodansky's great concerns is an alliance formed with Iran and Korea for a war against the United States. He reported that high-level delegations from Iran and North Korea met in January 1995 to discuss "forming an alliance" based on "clear and genuine political strategy." According to Bodansky, "The two delegations . . . reached agreements on such issues as nuclear weapons and going to war against the U.S."[12]

North Korea, Iran, and Iraq have all jumped on the highway of weapons of mass destruction and are ready to use them. How many other nations will want to travel that highway?

CYBERWAR

Among the most sinister forms of new weaponry are those controlled by computers. An entire new approach to warfare looms in the future, the so-called *cyberwar*. The computer arsenal will not feature armaments but the information systems of civilian and military operations. Though computer system advancements promise both convenience and rapid analysis, the increased reliance on such systems makes most countries vulnerable. For instance, if computer experts in one country could crash into the security codes of another country's stock market, perhaps they could bring the second nation to its knees and produce years of suffering for millions of people.

One 1995 *Time* cover was entitled "Cyberwar" and carried the subtitle: "The U.S. rushes to turn computers into tomorrow's weapons of destruction. But how vulnerable is the home front?" Writer Douglas Waller reported:

> In a secure vault in the U.S. army's super-secret Intelligence and Security Command in northern Virginia, Colonel Mike Taksley sketches the barest outlines of the new Armageddons. . . .
>
> The vision from the vault in Virginia is of "information warfare"—now the hottest concept in the halls of the Pentagon. Info warriors hope to transform the way soldiers fight. Their goal: to exploit the technological wonders of the late 20th century to launch rapid, stealthy, widespread and devastating attacks on the military and civilian infrastructure of an enemy.[13]

Cyberwar could be a very clean yet deadly battle. The soldiers would never see the horror of war—the blood and guts. They could just push a few buttons and say, "I was just doing my job." They would never understand the terror of war. Yet millions of lives could be destroyed and untold thousands die.

Already a generation of young people are growing up playing computer warfare games. They already know how to destroy the enemy. What would happen to civilization if real war became just another computer game? Safeguards in place may not be fail-safe after all.

NATIONS IN CONFLICT

It's not only that we live in a generation with the most destructive weapons in human history that makes the world such a dangerous place. But it's also that armed conflicts seem to be erupting all over the planet. During the five years ending in 1994, more than ninety armed conflicts broke out, "practically all of them within states (the most notable exception being Iraq-Kuwait) and involving more than 175 subnational groups and organizations," reports U.N. historian Mendez.[14]

So many armed conflicts are taking place around the world that it's almost impossible for the average person to keep up with them. Perhaps that's why Jesus said that before He returned there would be "wars and rumors of wars."

Two millennia ago Jesus predicted there would be "wars and rumors of wars" as nations and kingdoms rose up against one another. Those days seem to be upon us. And what are the effects of man falling to such a moral low? It appears that the more man is corrupted, the more nature convulses.

War today is producing refugees in unprecedented numbers around the globe. Mendez, the UN historian, wrote, "Military conflicts and natural disasters have, among other things, caused mass movements of refugees seeking haven in neighboring, and later in other, countries. More than 27 million refugees are now in flight."[15] With so many refugees on the move around the world, disease and famine are being given unprecedented opportunities to make new inroads in modern civilization.

In fact, rumblings from nature can no longer be ignored. In Part 2, we will hear what those rumblings mean for the approaching millennium.

Part Two

···

RUMBLINGS FROM NATURE

As the tools have been placed in man's hands to create chaos and destruction unknown to previous generations, nature seems to be lifting its head. The further man falls towards a moral low, the more nature violently reacts. Man was created to live in harmony with nature. But during these last days mankind and nature seem to be headed on a collision course.

The Bible predicted that nature would begin to convulse during the last days with plagues, famine, earthquakes, and natural disasters. New diseases have emerged at the close of the millennium that have been unknown in human history. In less than twenty years, the previously unknown virus that causes AIDS has encircled the globe, killing millions of people on every continent. Other unknown diseases have begun to make their way out of the rain forests and into the great urban centers of the world. Additionally, old diseases are returning with a vengeance. They've somehow found a way to adapt and resist present-day medical treatment.

Other natural phenomena are rumbling. Weather patterns seem to be shifting worldwide; major earthquakes threaten some of the great cities of the world; and the African continent is riddled with famine. One can't help but ask, "What's happening?"

Perhaps nature has begun to shout with a loud voice. The tiniest of microbes are warning mankind, "Enough of your violence, hatred, and pride. The time is at hand. The Creator will soon return!"

He becomes dizzy and utterly weak, and his spine goes
limp and nerveless and he loses all sense of balance. The room
is turning around and around. He is going into shock. He
leans over, head on his knees, and brings up an incredible
quantity of blood from his stomach and spills it onto the floor
with a gasping groan. He loses consciousness and pitches for-
ward onto the floor. The only sound is a choking in his throat
as he continues to vomit while unconscious. Then comes a
sound like a bedsheet being torn in half, which is the sound of
his bowels opening and venting blood . . . mixed with intesti-
nal lining. . . . Monet has crashed and is bleeding out.[1]

Richard Preston
The Hot Zone

....

Then I heard a mighty voice from the temple sanctuary
saying to the seven angels, Go and empty out on the earth the
seven bowls of God's wrath and indignation. So the first
[angel] went and emptied his bowl on the earth, and foul and
painful ulcers [sores] came on the people who were marked
with the stamp of the beast and who did homage to his
image.

Revelation 16:1, 2, Amplified Bible

Chapter Four

....

GLOBALIZATION OF INFECTIOUS DISEASES

India is a fascinating country. With almost 900 million inhabitants, it's the world's largest democracy. The people are intriguing; I especially enjoy interacting with the Indians because they are quite philosophical. And, yet, with all of the beauty of the country and dignity of the people, great poverty and disease permeate the nation.

In 1992 I visited the state of Andhra Pradesh for a pastors conference on Revival and Evangelism. More than one thousand Christian pastors gathered for the meetings. I was excited about what might take place with so many leaders in one conference. After arriving in Guntur, I headed toward my hotel; traveling by jet and train, my journey to the conference center in Guntur took almost two days. I was exhausted.

Yet I hadn't eaten on the ten-hour train ride because my Indian friends didn't think it was safe. I decided a quick meal in a local restaurant would be OK. After one bite of chicken, however, I knew that I shouldn't eat any more.

Discovering that the hotel room had air-conditioning lightened my concern; it even made up for the lack of running water and the primitive toilet facilities. Like many hotel rooms in the East, the toilet consisted of only a place to plant two feet and a hole in the floor. But the only thing that mattered that evening was that I had a cool place to sleep. That meant that I wouldn't have to fight mosquitoes all night. I fell sound asleep as soon as I hit the bed.

I woke up the next morning refreshed and ready to go. After some private time in prayer, I met an Indian friend in the hotel lobby, and we headed toward the bank to exchange money. I was scheduled to open the congress with my first message at about 11:00 A.M., but I began to feel weak after my visit to the bank. Instead of going to the conference center, I returned to the hotel for a little rest.

By the time my Indian friend arrived at the hotel to take me to the congress, I had a severe headache and felt very weak. I told him I didn't think that I had the strength to speak at the congress. "It's probably a bad case of jet lag. I just need to rest the first day. Please express my apologies to the pastors and tell them I will be there for my first session tomorrow morning."

Things rapidly got worse. The pain was so terrible that I began screaming. . . . I began sweating profusely. . . . I'm going to die here, *I thought.*

He left and I slept only one hour to awake with stomach cramps, soon followed by severe diarrhea. I had previously experienced traveler's stomach sickness, but this situation was much worse than that. I began vomiting and then came dry heaves. I knew that I was quickly becoming dehydrated. I picked up the phone and called the front desk and asked them to get me a doctor. No one spoke English. I kept saying, "I need a doctor!" And they kept replying, "You need water?"

The pain kept getting worse. Within thirty minutes the bathroom and bedroom had become a total mess because of my condition. The pain became almost unbearable. There was a knock on the door and I whispered, "Praise the Lord. A doctor is here." A young man walked in and spoke the only three English words he knew: "Room service—water."

"I need a doctor," I began to cry. "Please get me a doctor."

He smiled and responded, "Room service—water."

I wept in pain and said, "Please get me a doctor."

He left. I hoped he understood. But things rapidly got worse. The pain was so terrible that I began screaming. I was too weak to stand up and walk into the bathroom when I needed to. I began sweating profusely. The entire bed linens were soaked. *I'm going to die here*, I thought.

I called the front desk again and began to scream in pain, "I need a doctor! I need a doctor!" Five minutes later two young men from room service showed up in my room. Their eyes bulged out as they saw my condition and they immediately left. I didn't think I could endure the pain much longer, and I kept getting weaker by the minute.

In about an hour three men from the conference came to my room and were shocked at what they found. They tried to lift me out of the bed, but I had no strength and was totally dead weight. They called the men from room service for assistance. Six men wrapped me in my sheets and carried me downstairs as I screamed in pain. They loaded me into a taxi and rushed me to a mission hospital. As I was being transferred to the emergency room, life seemed to be leaving me, as I moved in and out of consciousness. The last thing I remember was a needle being stuck in my arm.

I awoke at about two in the morning and my strength was beginning to come back. I knew I would be all right. At the edge of my bed stood two Indian pastors praying for me. Although at eight that morning I was still very weak, I asked the nun, who was director of the hospital, to allow me to attempt to speak to the congress. She understood that I had come a long way for the meeting. The nurses unhooked the IV and put me in a taxi and sent me to the conference.

Although I was extremely weak, I preached and then was immediately taken back to the hospital by taxi. I was placed back on the IV I continued in such a manner until the conclusion of the congress.

At the hospital nurses would bring me a daily bucket of water. I used it to wash and shave because there wasn't running water in the emergency room. They normally kept a lid on the bucket in order to keep the mosquitoes from swarming around it. When I lifted the lid that last day in the hospital, my heart skipped a beat. Two dead rats were floating in the water. I skipped the shave and now had only one desire—to get home.

Although I was scheduled to speak in a few local churches following the conference, I asked my Indian friends for permission to leave the country early and return to the U.S. They were very gracious in excusing me. I was able to change my flight and catch a plane back to the U.S. immediately. One previous time I was hospitalized, in 1989 in Nigeria, and had the same response: I felt a great need to get home. I thought if I could get home, then any problem could be solved.

I never learned what caused the deadly attack on my system, though I believe it was a bacteria from the food. Fortunately, my sickness was not a highly infectious and lethal virus, and the airline readily accommodated me. But I've often wondered how many people with contagious diseases were on the flights I have taken.

VIRUSES: A DEADLY SCENARIO

Indeed, researchers and even novelists warn of such a

scenario spreading the deadly Ebola virus that dominated international health news in the mid-1990s. In *The Hot Zone*, writer Richard Preston described *true* events, including a Frenchman contracting the virus during a visit to Mount Elgon, which straddles Kenya and Uganda. The opening epigraph to this chapter describes the devastation to Charles Monet's body during the final minutes of his life.

Monet came to Nairobi on Kenya Airways after he fell ill, and Preston writes, "All of the earth's cities are connected by a web of airline routes. The web is a network. Once a virus hits the net, it can shoot anywhere in a day—Paris, Tokyo, New York, Los Angeles, wherever planes fly. Charles Monet and the life form inside him had entered the net."[2]

The virus did not spread through the airline net. If it had, devastation could have been global. The initial symptoms of Ebola virus include fever, followed by vomiting and diarrhea, nearly identical to my own malady.

That produces an important question. If someone who had just been infected with Ebola is a businessman or frequent flyer like I am, couldn't the airline allow him to catch an earlier flight home? If that happened, then the international network of cities could be entered by someone infected with the deadly virus.

During the Ebola outbreak in Zaire in 1995, tropical disease expert Robert Novak told the Associated Press, "We are never fully protected. We are not immune from things that float around the world. . . . You can't build a brick wall around America or take blood or stool samples (for disease screening) from everyone arriving at a U. S. port."[3]

Ironically, several other nations attempted just that after the Ebola outbreak in Zaire, screening for anyone coming from Zaire. Angola, Uganda, and Ivory Coast set up mandatory screening. Canada, Russia, Thailand, Brazil, Turkey, Lebanon, and the Philippines all implemented some sort of screening or ban on visas and/or flights from Zaire. France required passengers coming from Zaire to fill out questionnaires about contact with people infected with Ebola. Belgium even had doctors checking passengers boarding their three weekly flights to Brussels.[4] The nations of the world began to realize the potential devastating effect to humanity by the Ebola virus.

The Ebola virus . . . may be only the first of many deadly pestilences at the close of this century.

Though it's unlikely, Ebola or a similar virus could spread rapidly throughout the world. Because it kills people so quickly and is spread through intimate contact with an infected person, it most often burns out quickly. A virus that kills quickly is more easily contained because its devastation is experienced everywhere. Quarantines can be established such as was done in Zaire in 1995. Thus, the virus is left without a host through which it can spread. However, enough uncertainty surrounds Ebola and similar viruses to make health officials concerned such a virus could become pandemic—an outbreak of disease occurring over a large geographical area.

The Ebola virus appears to be a warning from nature. Jesus listed worldwide occurrences in Luke 21 that would transpire before He returns. He said that there would be "pestilences in various places, and fearful events" (verse 11). The Ebola virus certainly fits into that category. But it may be only the first of many deadly pestilences at the close of this century.

EBOLA: A VIRUS CASE STUDY

In order to understand the potential devastation of a deadly virus, let's study briefly the history of Ebola. There have been four major outbreaks of viruses in the Ebola family: Marburg in 1967, Ebola-Sudan and Ebola-Zaire in 1976, Ebola-Reston in 1989, and again Ebola-Zaire in 1995. Ebola is the name of a river that runs through the Zaire rain forest and into the Zaire (Congo) River. The name of the virus is derived from the river because of its emergence in the Ebola River region of Africa in the mid-1970s.

The Ebola virus family is called a filovirus. Researchers have learned that "the various strains of Ebola and its cousin Marburg are thin threads a little less than a thousandth of a millimetre long. From their shape they get the name filoviruses. There are seven proteins in the thread, wrapped around a coil of the chemical RNA on which the viral genes are recorded."[5] All three strains of the Ebola virus are similar and very deadly. Marburg and Ebola-Zaire are lethal to humans, but Ebola-Reston thus far has proven to be a killer of only monkeys and not humans.

Marburg

Marburg was first detected simultaneously in Germany and Yugoslavia in 1967, first appearing in three workers in Marburg, Germany. Within months the illness was found in six patients in Frankfurt and spread to Yugoslavia. In *The Coming Plague*, Laurie Garrett reported, "The thirty-one cases struck terror in European research circles because of the ferocity of the disease and its spread from patients to their health care providers." In its advanced stages Ebola caused the entire body to redden and patients to vomit blood. Within three weeks the patients' "skin peeled off. . . . Most succumb within sixteen days."[6]

The Marburg outbreak was traced to a shipment of monkeys that arrived in Belgrade, Yugoslavia, from Uganda. They were then shipped to Marburg and Frankfurt, Germany. The medical community was eventually able to contain the virus, but it seemed to go into hiding afterwards. Researchers attempted to find its origin, but were unable. Mystery surrounded the virus. It seemed to have vanished from the planet until 1975. Two young Australians hitchhiking through southern Africa came down with the dreaded disease. The young man died and his girlfriend survived. And the Marburg mystery remained.

Ebola-Sudan

The first Zaire outbreak of Ebola took place during September 1976. A man only referred to as Yu. G. by Ebola researchers came down with the deadly Ebola virus in Sudan two months prior to the Zaire outbreak. He had mistresses in his town and the disease began spreading rapidly. Preston described the devastating effects:

> The Sudan strain was more than twice as lethal as Marburg virus—its case-fatality rate was 50%. That is, fully half of the people who came down with it ended up dying and quickly. This was the same kind of fatality rate as was seen with the black plague during the Middle Ages. If the Ebola Sudan virus managed to spread out of central Africa, it might have entered Khartoum in a few weeks, penetrated Cairo a few weeks after that, and after that it would have hopped to Athens, New York, Paris, London, Singapore—it would have gone everywhere on the planet.[7]

Ebola-Zaire

When Ebola showed up in Zaire two months later, it was almost twice as deadly as Ebola-Sudan, killing more than 80 percent of those infected with it. It spread through fifty-five villages simultaneously. It first showed up in Yambuku in a hospital run by Belgian nuns. A schoolteacher who received an injection at the hospital first came down with Ebola-Zaire. It began spreading rapidly through the villages surrounding Yambuku. It killed people who had received injections from the hospital. It then spread to family members.

One of the nuns at the hospital then came down with Ebola. She was taken by a priest to Kinshasa, Zaire's capital. Then a nurse at Kinshasa's largest hospital came down with the virus. As word began to spread, Zaire's President Mobutu Sese Seko set a quarantine around the "hot zone" surrounding Yambuku and also the hospital in Kinshasa that had seen the virus. The virus then withdrew and went again into hiding. Researchers were sent to Zaire to try to find the natural host or reservoir for the virus. They traveled through Zaire's rain forest attempting to catch and collect every kind of animal or insect. But they were unable to find a species that carried the Ebola virus. But Ebola-Zaire also remained a mystery—hidden somewhere in the forests of Zaire and Sudan.

Experts could only wait and wonder when it might reappear. They had seen the devastation of Marburg, and now Ebola-Zaire was even worse.

In 1995 Ebola-Zaire showed up again, this time in Kitwik, Zaire. Approximately three hundred people died from the killer virus. Interestingly, Ebola-Zaire appeared shortly after the release of Preston's nonfiction book, *The Hot Zone,* and almost simultaneously with the opening of the fiction movie *Outbreak.*

After Ebola-Zaire broke out in 1995, *Newsweek* asked Preston, "How concerned should we be about the outbreak in Zaire?" He responded,

Ebola has reared its ugly head again, and one of the big concerns is that we still don't know where it lives in nature. It is a traveller. It is a species jumper. . . . We don't think it's going to go out of Zaire because people don't live long when they get Ebola. But it's a classic warning.[8]

Ebola-Reston

Another strain of Ebola caused shock waves among researchers when it appeared in Reston, Virginia, just outside Washington, D.C. It is this strain to which Preston devoted much of his book. The movie *Outbreak* based its story on Preston's book, but the movie was completely fictional. In the movie, the virus was deadly to humans. However, in real life the Ebola-Reston virus did not prove to be fatal to people.

In 1989 a group of crab-eating monkeys were imported from the Philippines to a facility in Reston, Virginia. Some of the monkeys became ill and suddenly and mysteriously started dying. Samples of monkey tissue were sent to the nearby USAMRIID, the U.S. Army's center for research on infectious diseases. Researchers at the army center were shocked to find a filovirus—a strain of Ebola. Though the monkeys were killed, one disturbing aspect was that the monkey tissue initially was inspected at Biosafety Level 3 without the "space suits" required for study at Level 4, which protects against the deadly, mysterious, and incurable viruses being studied there. That could have been tragic for those studying the tissue, and it could have resulted in a hot zone appearing in the suburbs of one of the most influential and powerful cities in the world!

Interestingly, Ebola-Reston appears to be non-lethal to humans. Although a couple of people seemed to have been infected with the virus at the monkey facility, they didn't die nor suffer Ebola-like symptoms. Experts believe that

Ebola-Reston won't kill humans, but they're not absolutely sure of it.[9]

Some experts believe that those monkeys were imported to the Philippines from Africa. The African monkeys probably infected the Philippine monkeys with the Ebola virus. The Ebola virus more than likely adapted while in the Philippines. The new strain looks very much like Ebola-Zaire and kills monkeys just like Ebola-Zaire, but for some reason it has proven to be non-fatal to humans thus far. Experts really don't know what it might do because it also went into hiding. The mystery around Ebola-Reston remains.

UNANSWERED QUESTIONS

The mysterious strains of the Ebola virus have left us with serious questions to ponder. Where did they come from? Where did they go? What is the natural reservoir (animal or insect that acts as its host without being killed by the virus)? Will there eventually be a strain of Ebola-Reston that is fatal to humans? How many other unknown lethal viruses are waiting in the rain forests of the world and ready to jump species? How long would it take for such a virus to enter the international network of air travel and bring devastation to humanity?

It seems as though Ebola has given a wake-up call to mankind at the close of the twentieth century. Jesus spoke of these kinds of diseases appearing before He returned. John foresaw such deadly outbreaks when he wrote the book of Revelation. It appears that nature is beginning to raise its head and cry out for God's judgment.

OTHER DANGEROUS VIRUSES

But Ebola isn't the only or even the greatest concern for researchers today. A host of diseases has taken center stage on the world scene during this critical moment of history. Some are ancient ones that scientists thought they had removed from the planet. Others are new and deadly. Still other viruses have built a resistance to drugs that used to destroy them.

During the 1950s scientists were celebrating because of discoveries that produced vaccines and cures for some of the most ravaging diseases known to mankind. But as the century comes to a close, that celebration has turned to grave concern.

One of the most powerful agencies in the world in attempting to research and control the spread of disease is the U.S. Centers for Disease Control (CDC), an agency that in 1995 had allotted $130 million for infectious disease control. In a fascinating report on the CDC, *U. S. News and World Report* investigated the specter of disease at the close of the twentieth century.

> New plagues as well as old diseases are on the rampage. AIDS, Lyme Disease, Legionnaires' disease and the hantavirus seem to have appeared out of nowhere. Rabies and tuberculosis are back with a vengeance; TB swept through a high school in Los Angeles last October, infecting a third of the students—including 12 who contacted a strain of bacterium that is resistant to all standard treatments.
>
> . . . What scares people at the CDC even more than exotic diseases are the mundane microbes, once easily quashed with antibiotics, that have started defeating even the newest and most powerful drugs.[10]

The magazine listed five threats that frighten researchers the most: (1) *"Superbacteria,"* new resistant strains, such as the deadly staph bug found in hospitals that is immune to every antibiotic but one; (2) *new diseases,* such as Ebola, that rival AIDS; (3) *re-emerging dis-*

eases, including a highly resistant form of tuberculosis; (4) *contaminated food and water;* and (5) *influenza.*[11]

Science can define, experiment with, and build upon nature, but it cannot change nature itself. And nature appears to be erupting like a violent volcano in these last few years of the millennium.

Even as this book went to press in early 1996, scientists warned that a new virus could become a pandemic soon, killing millions of people worldwide. A *USA Today* cover story concluded with this ominous warning: "A flu virus no one has ever been exposed to, one that can move swiftly, causing illness and death, social chaos and political disaster around the globe, could be incubating right now in a remote part of China."[12]

One researcher attributes the spread of both old and new diseases to several of the facts we cited in the introduction, including transportation, communication, and technological information. Stephen Morse, assistant professor of virology at the Rockefeller University and chairman of the 1989 Conference on Emerging Viruses, gave four reasons for the spread of infectious diseases today: (1) *changes in human demographics and behavior,* with the emergency of HIV due to promiscuous sex and recreational drug use a classic example; (2) *international travel and commerce;* (3) *technology and industry;* and (4) *microbial adaptation and change.*[13]

For years we've thought that science could correct any problem facing humanity. And science has benefited mankind tremendously. Science can define, experiment with, and build upon nature, but it cannot change nature itself. And nature appears to be erupting like a violent volcano in these last few years of the millennium. For all of the progress that humanity has made, nature seems to be protesting, adapting, and striking back.

The world is rapidly changing. As progress marches forward, mankind has deluded itself into thinking that we hold destiny in our own hands. However, the march of history is directed by the Creator and Sustainer of the universe. We could not have come to this unique and critical moment in history without the sovereign hand of God.

In Revelation, the Bible's final book, the description of the end times before Christ's return to earth includes a picture of seven bowls of God's wrath. The first bowl of wrath appears to be the worldwide globalization of painful and destructive diseases. "The first angel went and poured out his bowl on the land, and ugly and painful sores broke out on the people who had the mark of the beast and worshiped his image" (Revelation 16:2).

The *New England Journal of Medicine* began an article on the spread of infectious disease in Somalia by referring to the book of Revelation: "The Four Horsemen of the Apocalypse—War, Famine, Pestilence, and Death—ride the arid plains of Somalia."[14] It would only take one act of God's judgment to cause an infectious pandemic disease to spread rapidly worldwide so that it would mirror exactly that which the Bible speaks about in Revelation.

But nature has already given a warning much more severe than Ebola or any of the viruses described in this chapter. It could possibly become the most devastating killer that man has ever come in contact with. Some scientists believe that 25 million people will be murdered by this small virus by the year 2000.

The first AIDS cases are believed to have occurred in the late 1960s. By the mid-1970s, changes in modern air travel brought HIV to the rest of the world. Jumbo jets and decreased airfares produced dramatic increases in travel to and from Central Africa, distributing HIV widely. As four-teenth-century travel had to become rapid and efficient enough to bring plague from Asia, modern jet travel had to expand to Central Africa to bring HIV to the rest of the world. The earliest sites were probably central Europe and Haiti. The link to the United States appears to be homosexual males vacationing in the area of Port-au-Prince, Haiti. From there, HIV infection was carried to those areas with the largest con-centrations of homosexual males, New York and San Fran-cisco. . . .

The next group infected with HIV were intravenous drug users. . . . The next wave of the epidemic, which is only begin-ning, is the spread of HIV infection to the sexual partners of bisexual males and intravenous drug users. . . . The final wave of the epidemic, which has not yet begun, will be when HIV infection is spread widely into the remainder of the pop-ulation.[1]

Robert M. Swenson
Professor of medicine and microbiology
at Temple University Health Science Center.

....

There will be great earthquakes, famines and pestilences in various places, and fearful events and great signs from heaven.

Luke 21:11

Chapter Five

....

GLOBALIZATION
OF HIV

Before leaving on an overseas speaking trip, I got a call from a friend asking me to pray for Joseph (not his real name), who was infected with the human immunodeficiency virus (HIV). The virus had finally reached the stage of AIDS, and my friend Joseph was now seriously ill in the hospital. I did pray, but I admit I was shocked to see Joseph in a local shopping mall just days after I returned from the trip.

"Joseph, it's great to see you," I said. "How are you doing?"

"Do you want the Christian answer or the real one?" he bitterly retorted.

"Whichever one you want to give, Joseph. It's a sincere question. Before I left on my trip overseas, I heard that you were really sick. I've been praying for you. I was surprised to see you up and around."

Joseph apologized. "Look, Sammy, this is getting rough. I'm really very sick and everyone expects me to just go around saying, 'Praise the Lord!' I can't do it. I'm really hurting."

We visited another twenty minutes and he had to leave. I tried to understand how he felt. My heart really went out to Joseph. He and I both grew up in and around Baton Rouge, Louisiana. He was young and an extremely talented keyboard player. He played several years for a television evangelist, but during that time he chose to visit a homosexual bar. He met a guy there and had sexual relations with him. Not long after his liaison he learned that he had been infected with HIV. His life came tumbling down. He decided to leave Baton Rouge and later moved to San Antonio. Shortly afterwards I met Joseph. It was while living in San Antonio that he deeply repented of his sin and surrendered himself to Christ.

God forgave him and transformed his life. But the virus had already developed fully into AIDS. Joseph gave himself the next couple of years to sharing the love of Jesus with those who were infected with HIV. But the virus continued to take its toll on him. Not long after our encounter in the mall, Joseph died. After hearing the news, my heart broke. Joseph had so much talent and potential.

I began to reflect on what had happened to Joseph. How did a young man like Joseph die of a disease that was virtually unknown to mankind just twenty years earlier? Where did this sickness come from? But more important than that question, where is it headed? How many lives will be destroyed by it?

THE ORIGIN OF HIV

There are not a lot of concrete answers to those questions. Scientists seem to disagree about the origin of AIDS, although most believe that it came out of Africa. One area in Africa especially hit hard with AIDS parallels a highway that winds from Zaire through Uganda to Kenya. Many people call it the AIDS Highway because there's such a high incidence of AIDS along the route. For many years it had not been much more than a dirt path. But as the region progressed, a highway was built that would become a major commercial route linking the three nations. Truck drivers who had sexual relations with prostitutes along the route became natural carriers of HIV. They brought it out of the rain forests and into the major cities. From there the virus was able to spread through the international network of air travel.

AIDS has produced a number of moral and ethical questions. To a great extent it has become such a politicized issue that it's sometimes difficult to get straightforward answers to many questions.

During December 1994, I preached at a citywide evangelistic meeting in Uganda in the region of the AIDS Highway. Thousands of people gathered in an open field every afternoon for the meetings. One afternoon I asked the crowd, "How many of you have a close friend or a relative who has AIDS?" Almost everyone in the field lifted a hand. There was virtually no one in the area that had not been touched, at least emotionally, by the deadly disease.

In Africa, AIDS remains primarily a disease spread by heterosexual intercourse. In fact, several married African women posed one of the most difficult questions I heard during my visit to Uganda: "If we think our husbands are promiscuous, should we have sexual relations with them? If they get AIDS from a mistress or a prostitute, then we may end up with AIDS and die."

AIDS has produced a number of moral and ethical questions. To a great extent it has become such a politicized issue that it's sometimes difficult to get straightforward answers to many questions. Laurie Garrett wrote:

Because of the legacy of blame, accusation, and exaggeration concerning AIDS in Africa it was impossible to have an apolitical, "pure science" discussion of the origins of the human immunodeficiency virus during the 1980s. . . . Still there would remain in the 1990s a decided timidity in AIDS academic and policy circles about broaching the subject of the origins of the global pandemic. The official line of the World Health Organization, first enunciated by Assad in 1985, would remain the agency's position in 1994: AIDS emerged simultaneously on at least three continents. Few scientists accepted that position, recognizing it for what it was—a political compromise. But publicly they went along with WHO's stance because it was politically too dangerous to do otherwise.[2]

African nations did not want blame placed on them for the pandemic of AIDS, and homosexuals in the West did not want to accept blame for introducing HIV to the Western world. So because many researchers don't want to be known as "racist" or "homophobic," the origin of AIDS remains a debated subject. But as Kenneth Kaunda, former president of Zambia, said in 1987, "What is more important than knowing where the disease came from is where it is going."[3]

Nevertheless, there are generally two accepted theories concerning the origin of AIDS. One theory is that AIDS was around for a long time. Perhaps people died of AIDS deep in the rain forests, but because of lack of transportation and communication, it wasn't known to the rest of the world's population. The other theory is that it has only recently jumped species (from monkeys to man).[4] No matter which theory proves to be true, one thing is for certain. Its worldwide spread has been due in part to the mobility of people that has accelerated during the last half of this century.

We look at HIV in this chapter neither to be sensational nor to assign blame. Instead we will consider how the virus, manifested as AIDS, resembles the biblical prophecy of pestilence and plagues during the last days. And we will consider what can be done about this virus. First let's look at the nature of HIV and its impact on individuals and society.

GOD, SCIENCE, AND MORAL BEHAVIOR

For the sake of integrity, I must say that I make no claims to be a scientist nor an expert on AIDS. I have researched what scientists and experts are saying about AIDS. I have and will continue to quote from some of those scientists. However, some of them may disagree with some of the conclusions that I have drawn. Those conclusions are based on my observations of scientific research and how they resemble the fulfillment of biblical prophecy. In much of my research, I have discovered that a number of scientific writers refer to preachers who declare that AIDS is a judgment from God as being "bizarre" and "extreme."

If a person attempts to prove scientifically that AIDS has resulted from God's judgment, critics would be correct in saying that theory is bizarre. In order to prove scientifically the "God's judgment" theory, one must prove three things: (1) God exists, (2) God has moral character, and (3) the basis for moral behavior has been revealed in the Bible, and man will be held accountable for that behavior. That would be impossible to prove scientifically.

But in the same manner it would be impossible to disprove the reality of God and the truth of Scriptures scientifically. It would be just as bizarre to state that based on scientific evidence, there is proof that God does not exist or that He doesn't have moral character. As a matter of fact, a number of scientists believe that the orderliness of nature and the universe is evidence of a master creator and designer.

It takes as much faith and maybe even more faith to

argue against God and His revelation of His nature, character, and moral design of man as it does to believe in God and the Bible. I make no apologies for my belief in the God of the Bible and what He declares as moral truth. I believe the evidence strongly favors belief in God and His moral truth. My observations are simply comparative statements of what scientists are saying about AIDS and what the Bible says about the consequences of immoral behavior and what will transpire in the last days.

WHAT IS AIDS?

Acquired immune deficiency syndrome, or AIDS, is a condition where the immune system collapses, allowing a number of serious illnesses into the body that will weaken and eventually kill the person. The condition of AIDS is produced by the human immunodeficiency virus, or HIV. The *Field Guide to Germs* describes it as "the third of five retroviruses discovered since 1980 (there are undoubtedly more)." It's a transcriptase, which converts viral RNA into a DNA copy that becomes part of the host cell's DNA.[5]

HIV attaches itself to the T-cell, the cell that stimulates our immune system, causing it to ward off other diseases. Specifically, HIV enters the T-cell and then begins to transcribe itself into the DNA of that cell. New T-cells then have the same genetic code of the HIV-infected cell. Over the next two to fifteen years the immune system fights a long but losing battle against the AIDS virus. As the immune system is overwhelmed by the virus, other opportunistic diseases attack the infected person. Those diseases often become the human killers.

AIDS AND DISEASE

A variety of diseases appear in AIDS patients, the most common being pneumocystis carinii pneumonia, a parasitic infection of the lungs. Also very common in AIDS patients is cytomegalovirus (CMV) infection. Extremely common among AIDS patients and the general homosexual population, this herpes virus causes blindness, pneumonia, colitis, and esophagitis.[6]

AIDS has promoted a resurgence of diseases that scientists thought they were conquering. For example, researchers felt they were gaining control over tuberculosis. However, reported cases of TB increased 20 percent between 1985 and 1992, and surveys in TB clinics showed that 47 percent of the U.S.-born patients between ages twenty-five and forty-four were HIV positive.[7] The January 18, 1995, issue of the *Journal of the American Medical Association* stated that tuberculosis may affect 90 million people and kill 30 million worldwide. Developing countries will account for 95 percent of TB cases.[8]

What makes HIV so dangerous is its ability to suppress the immune system; that enables other diseases to enter the body and kill the individual. But equally dangerous is HIV's status as a slow progressing virus. Unlike Ebola, where symptoms show up immediately and the virus kills within two weeks, HIV enters quietly, with only minor symptoms at first. Then the disease begins its fight with the T-cells, which can last for years before a major problem is discovered. Consequently, the carrier of the virus has the opportunity to infect others before knowing he's infected. Leading AIDS researcher Jonathan Mann described the implications:

> After infection a person may remain symptom-free for years. An unknown proportion of infected people do experience an early, brief, mononucleosis-like illness with fever, malaise and possibly a skin rash. . . . From that point on an average of eight or nine years may pass before AIDS is fully developed. The fatality rate for AIDS, once it has been developed, is very high; it may reach 100 per cent. [9]

A GLOBAL VIRUS

This can partly explain why this small virus has stunned governments around the world, causing billions of dollars to be spent on research and treatment. According to the *New York Times*, "the oldest documented case of AIDS from which HIV has been traced is a 1976 case in Zaire. . . ."[10] From that documented case until today the AIDS virus has exploded on the world scene. By January 3, 1995, the World Health Organization's (WHO) estimates were as follows:

- 1,025,073 reported cases of AIDS
- 4.5 million estimated cases of AIDS
- 18 million estimated infections of HIV[11]

Within twenty years the virus spread from one person to 18 million worldwide. That's an incredible spread of the deadly virus. It took only one infected person to enter the worldwide web of air travel. Then the virus was able to sow its seeds of death and devastation throughout Africa, Europe, North America, Asia, South America, and Australia. Seemingly no nation is exempt from its quiet but destructive attack on the human immune system. "The AIDS epidemic is out of control," declared Mann in 1992 while chairing the Amsterdam conference on AIDS. He added: "We now recognize the painful reality that existing approaches to prevention—as remarkable as some efforts have been—will not be sufficient to stem the pandemic."[12]

Governments and scientists alike seem helpless as they attempt to stem the tide of the rapidly spreading AIDS virus. Just how far has the virus spread? Why can't the greatest minds in the world seem to find a vaccine or cure for the deadly virus? The United States has more reported cases of AIDS than any other country in the world, and the number continues to rise. Most Americans seem to think it's a homosexual disease. But as African victims will tell us, AIDS is a heterosexual disease as well. Many North Americans have a rude awakening coming. The Centers for Disease Control and Prevention in Atlanta has found that "nearly three-quarters of the 40,000 new infections with HIV, the virus that causes AIDS, last year were among addicts. . . . Maybe as much as half of the new infections among heterosexuals are occurring in relation to crack cocaine."[13]

The AIDS virus has taken a new twist in the United States. It has moved from primarily infecting the homosexual population to infecting drug users. Some researchers now fear that it will spread rapidly among sex partners of addicts and then possibly into the general population.

This virus has the potential of being the greatest killer that man has ever faced. All of our human resources, intelligence, and technology don't seem to be able to stop this tiny virus.

Although the United States is the most infected nation with HIV, sub-Saharan Africa is the most infected region of the world. The director of AIDS research at the National Institutes of Health, William E. Paul, said:

Human immunodeficiency virus, the causative agent of AIDS, has penetrated virtually every population on the globe. More than 17 million children, women, and men are infected, with the largest number being in sub-Saharan Africa. The epidemic is rapidly gathering force in Asia where the number of new cases of AIDS increased eightfold in a single year. In several Asian nations, a public health disaster is in the making.[14]

Several scientific journals and news articles have been warning of the rapidly growing worldwide AIDS pandemic. One *New Scientist* magazine headline in 1994 read, "France's AIDS Time Bomb," and the article detailed the alarming rate of the growth of AIDS in France.[15] Five months later the journal reported that 2.5 million people had been "infected in Asia, but WHO estimates that this will increase to 10 million by 2000."[16] The *Los Angeles Times* reported that in South Africa those who "tested positive for HIV has rocketed from 5,000 cases in 1990 to an estimated 1.8 million."[17]

FINDING A CURE

Africa, Asia, America—thousands are dying annually and millions continue to be infected. And no cure or vaccine is likely in the near future. This virus has the potential of being the greatest killer that man has ever faced. All of our human resources, intelligence, and technology don't seem to be able to stop this tiny virus.

Finding a cure will not be easy. The virus mutates quickly, frustrating researchers' efforts to develop a vaccine. By the time a researcher is able to develop a vaccine for the virus, he discovers that it had changed, mutating into a new subtype. The vaccine is now for a form of the virus that no longer exits. Jose' Esparza of WHO says, "Unless a vaccine can protect against several subtypes, it will be useless." He continued to express his concern about our inability to find a solution to the AIDS virus, stating, "Every day we wait, we lose another 5,000 or 10,000 people."[18] If you take Mr. Esparza's figures into the next decade, we could at that time be losing people in the millions.

The present social and moral conditions have made humanity susceptible to what could be the greatest killer to ever visit mankind. No doubt the quick mobility of large groups of people has enabled HIV to spread rapidly and bring such devastation. But the moral climate in the West has also created fertile soil for such a virus to take root and blossom around the world. Many post–World War II "baby boomers" decided to forsake the faith of their forefathers and leave traditional Judeo/Christian values during the mid to late 1960s. This resulted in a sexual revolution that has left the West with an increasing rate of divorce, drug abuse, and sexually transmitted diseases. (Of course, many of those infected with HIV were innocent victims as well, including spouses and children of AIDS carriers and hemophiliacs who received transfusions of infected blood.)

Recently I spoke to a national student conference in the United States. Before I could challenge this generation of young people to have moral courage, I knew that I needed to apologize to them. I asked their forgiveness because my generation decided that it was OK to "expand our minds" with drugs and experiment with sex. Consequently, "Generation X" has to face the one of the worst pandemics ever known to humanity. We have brought civilization to the brink of the valley of the shadow of death.

Garrett has listed social conditions in the 1970s throughout the world that gave HIV ample opportunity to develop into a worldwide pandemic. She wrote,

> Multiple partner sexual activity increased dramatically among gay North American and European men and among African urban heterosexuals; needles were introduced to the African continent on a massive scale for medical purposes, and then resupplied so poorly that their constant reuse on hundreds, even thousands, of people was necessary; heroin use, coupled with amphetamines and cocaine, soared in the industrialized world; waves of other sexually transmitted diseases swept across the same regions, lowering affected individuals' resistance to disease and creating . . . portals of entry for the virus.[19]

Several elements that Garrett mentions reflect moral choices: homosexual behavior, sexual promiscuity, and use of illicit drugs. Interestingly the Bible admonishes people to avoid such activities. Indeed, when God created man and woman, He also instituted marriage, intending that one man and one woman share sexual intimacy in that institution alone. But my generation forsook those cherished values. Live-in relationships became popular in the 1970s. Homosexuals came "out of the closet." Drug abuse rose as a generation sang, "I can't get no satisfaction." The next generation now faces increased divorce, an acceleration of crime, and deadly diseases.

AIDS is simply nature shouting from the rain forests that life suffers when people contradict the principles by which the universe was created. . . . Whether it is sexual permissiveness in the West, polygamy in Africa, or drug abuse around the world, nature seems to be answering man's violation of God's natural order.

One solution offered by the federal government and much of the "baby boom" generation (which is much more educated in the 1990s) has been sexual protection, rather than sexual abstinence. "Don't worry, guys," society tells teens and young adults in "Generation X." "Just wear condoms and we'll try to pass legislation to get new needles for your drugs. And don't let any of those Bible thumpers put you on a guilt trip about what you are doing."

The students broke out in applause when I asked their forgiveness. As members of "Generation X," they recognize that my generation has grossly failed the next one. Unless there is a great spiritual awakening and moral renewal in this generation, we have brought civilization to the edge of severe judgment. AIDS is simply nature shouting from the rain forests that life suffers when people contradict the principles by which the universe was created. AIDS is not some weird aberration of nature. It's a wake-up call. Whether it is sexual permissiveness in the West, polygamy in Africa, or drug abuse around the world, nature seems to be answering man's violation of God's natural order.

According to the Bible that order is simply one man and one woman committed to each other for a lifetime. It's building a family where love, peace, security, and fulfillment are found within that unit. It's the old-time, old-fashioned, pre-AIDS view of the family. But you may protest, saying, "Wait a minute. I know someone that has AIDS but also cherishes that view of life." Please understand that I'm not speaking of individuals, but rather of society as a whole. There are many innocent victims of AIDS. But society to a great extent has adopted a philosophy of relativism, which condones any behavior and at the same time ridicules those who hold to traditional biblical values.

A wise friend once told me, "When you find yourself off track, then retrace your steps to the place where you took the wrong turn. Then get back on the right track." That's what I believe that we must do as a society. There aren't enough condoms or new needles in the world to stop nature's violent eruption.

Nature seems to be speaking loudly and clearly that mankind cannot continue down the slippery slope of immoral behavior. We cannot continue to ignore God's principles of living and not face the consequences. Even many scientists will agree that we have brought the epidemic upon ourselves. Joe McCormick, head of the CDC special pathogens investigations, has said, "Human beings have done it to themselves. And that's not moralistic, it's just a fact."[20]

AIDS AS PESTILENCE

As a deadly, worldwide disease propagated mainly by the behavior of humans, AIDS looks like the end-times pestilence described by the Bible in Revelation 16:2, "The first angel went and poured out his bowl on the land, and ugly and painful sores broke out on the people who had the mark of the beast and worshipped his image." The pestilence of the great period of tribulation is directly related to human behavior.

As a disaster we initiated, AIDS resembles a biblical pestilence. In the Old Testament, pestilences often were a sign of God's impending judgment. *Nelson's Bible Dictionary* notes, "The words *pestilence* (Jer. 21:6; KJV) and *plague* (Ex. 11:1) seem to refer to contagious diseases of epidemic proportions which God sent occasionally as instruments of judgment upon His people as well as pagan nations of the world."[21] In the New Testament (Luke 21:11) Jesus uses the word *pestilences* to describe the world situation immediately prior to His return. In Luke 21:11 God's judgment appears to be coming through earthquakes, famine, and pestilences.

Interestingly, *Vine's Expository Dictionary of New Testament Words* defines *pestilence* (*lolmos* in the Greek) as "any deadly malicious malady."[22] In Revelation 16:2 the apostle John describes diseases producing terrible and painful sores being poured upon the world because of man's rebellion against God. The rapid and deadly spread of AIDS has all the characteristics of a latter-day pestilence: contagious disease, deadly malady, worldwide spread, painful sores, and man's rebellion against God's law.

I'm not saying that AIDS is the fulfillment of that passage. I'm simply saying that AIDS found its way to every
corner of the planet because of immoral behavior patterns
adopted by a large segment of society. Whatever one
believes about the "mark of the beast" and "worshipping
his image," those actions represent disobedience to God's
moral and righteous laws, making people open to a painful
pestilence. AIDS seems to be nature's way of acting and
speaking prophetically like John the Baptist, who was "a
voice crying in the wilderness saying, 'Repent, for the kingdom of heaven is at hand.'"

The trend is quite clear—the 1960s to the 80s. . . . there has been a fivefold increase in the frequency of great natural disasters, and a threefold increase in total economic losses.[1]

M'Hamed Essaafi
United Nations Disaster Relief Coordinator

There will be great earthquakes, famines and pestilences in various places, and fearful events and great signs from heaven.
Luke 21:11

Chapter Six

NATURAL
DISASTERS

A major snowstorm in March 1993 swept over the East Coast of the United States while I was addressing Bible college students in suburban Washington, D.C. I awoke the next morning to a winter wonderland—and news that classes had been canceled due to the heavy snow. The students' conference was over, and I knew that I should get to the airport as soon as possible. All the major highways to Washington National Airport were closed, but I still had one option: the train. With only a few people on the train and no one on the highways, I figured few people would board the jet this Friday and I could take an earlier flight.

Was I ever wrong! When I arrived at Washington's National Airport, there was total chaos. What I didn't know was that this storm was being called by news commentators "the storm of the century." It closed airports across the entire eastern seaboard of the United States. Travelers were stranded all over the East. As I looked at the maze of frustrated and weary people, I thought, *One act of nature, and the most technologically sophisticated nation on the earth comes to a halt.* (Another monster blizzard paralyzed airports on the East Coast in January 1996, halting air traffic for almost three days.)

I realized that we were not nearly as powerful as we thought. News reports stated, "With major airports from Atlanta to Boston closed for hours at a time, there was a domino effect. Travelers in Honolulu and Europe, including people who weren't trying to go anywhere near the East Coast, were affected. Around a quarter of the USA's normal air traffic never left the ground on the 13th and 14th [of March]."[2]

SHIFTING WEATHER PATTERNS

When I finally caught my flight, a weary traveler next to me said, "The weather sure seems to be strange these days." That wasn't the first time that I've heard that statement. The last several years I've often heard people from many countries say the same thing. More importantly, many meteorologists and scientists are beginning to say weather patterns are shifting worldwide. The world's climate may be changing. Certainly the 1990s have been a turbulent decade for weather in the United States and around the world.

What's happening? Why are we experiencing such turbulent times of weather?

The *USA Today Weather Almanac* has reported, "Since 1992 the United States has experienced its costliest hurricane, the winter storm of the century, the worst flooding in the history of the Mississippi and Missouri river valleys, one of our coldest winters, record breaking heat and the beginning of a drought in the West."[3] In 1995 Britain's *Economist* magazine noted, "All over the world, there is something odd about the weather."[4]

How bad is it? Consider 1995 alone. By late October 1995 meteorologists almost ran out of letters in the alphabet to be used for names of tropical hurricanes during the relatively brief hurricane season. The 1995 tropical storm season was the second most active season since record keeping began in 1871.[5] Heat waves killed scores in Chicago and throughout the midwestern United States, leaving the Great Plains reeling only two years after the worst flooding in a century of the Mississippi, America's largest river. Meanwhile, torrential rains flooded much of California. What's happening? Why are we experiencing such turbulent times of weather?

Cause 1: Global Warming

Scientists disagree on the answer to the above question, offering three different explanations. Some argue that the strange weather patterns result from global warming. This is a hotly debated topic among scientists and politicians. In 1992 leaders from around the world gathered in Rio de Janeiro for an Earth Summit. Their first order of business was "to sign a treaty to curtail a buildup of gaseous pollutants in the atmosphere . . . which are feared to lead to a rapid warming of the atmosphere." However, controversy permeated the congress, and "the world's richest nation voiced the same concern as the world's poorest nations: that measures taken to ameliorate the threat posed by global warming would create a serious impediment to economic growth."[6]

British data released in 1996 support the idea of an ongoing warm-up. Based on land and sea measurements from around the world, the British found the earth's surface temperature in 1995 was the warmest since record keeping began in 1856.[7] In America, the director of the NASA Goddard Institute predicted that a new global record would be reached before 2000. James Hansen also blamed much of what he calls a "century-long global warming trend" on human influence, especially the emission of such heat-trapping gases as carbon dioxide.[8]

Among the many potential effects of global warming are warmer rivers and streams that would be "more hospitable to germs like those that cause cholera [and] disease carriers such as the Aedes Aegypti mosquito . . . making illnesses such as malaria more widespread."[9]

The great leaders of the world find themselves at a stalemate over global warming, wondering about its actual impact and the appropriate responses. Is man responsible for the disruption of the natural order of creation, as Hansen and others suggest? No absolutely positive answer has yet been given to that question. However, many observers feel that it's urgent to know the answers to those questions or irreversible damage could be done to civilization itself.

I took a one-day trip down the Amazon River in 1995, accompanied by an elderly minister of the gospel who had traveled the Amazon forty years. I asked him what changes he had seen in the Amazon region over the years.

"The invasion of people," he answered. "There are many people traveling into the region that were never before here. The more that people have come into the region, the more the animals have fled."

While we were walking through a jungle area, he said, "Look, where are the animals? They're gone. They have retreated further into the jungles with the advent of people." Then he pointed to a pasture where cattle were grazing. "That's unnatural," he continued. "The Amazon isn't farmland. It's a jungle. Anywhere you see farms and pastureland, you can know that man has changed the natural environment of the Amazon."

When we arrived back at the boat, I could see hundreds of trees that had been cut down and acres of land that had been cleared.

In late 1995, *Time* magazine reported,

Every year hordes of Brazil's land-starved peasants press deeper and deeper into the Amazon rain forest, clearing patches of earth by putting torches to the trees. It's a largely self-defeating exercise, since the forest soil is unsuitable for farming. After a few seasons, when the land plays out, the peasants move on, clearing more ground and cutting a swatch of devastation across one of the world's most precious ecosystems.[10]

Some scientists believe that the deforestation of the Amazon and other equatorial rain forests is playing a pivotal role in global warming. They feel that irreversible damage is being done by man to some of the most important regions of the world which will continue to produce dramatic changes in weather patterns.

Cause 2: Volcanic Eruption in the Philippines

However, other scientists are skeptical of such arguments. They believe that there are two other primary reasons for the unusual weather patterns around the world during the 1990s. They refer to the eruption of Mount Pinatubo in 1991 in the Philippines and to the El Niño that began during the same year. They occurred so close in time that scientists have had a difficult time discerning which one has more dramatically affected weather patterns.

Mount Pinatubo exploded in June 1991 and covered portions of the island with ash and darkened the skies for days. The *USA Today Weather Almanac* called the volcanic eruption the beginning of "a long global climate experiment that scientists never could have created." The volcano pushed material into the earth's atmosphere and "about 4.7 percent more solar energy than normal was reflected away from the Earth."[11] As a result scientists believe that created a cooling of the earth that has thrown nature off balance and produced strange weather patterns.

Cause 3: Changed Air Flow from El Niño

The other factor cited for strange weather patterns is El Niño. In 1991 this warm air flow from the Pacific Ocean lasted longer than normal. El Niño occurs every three to seven years and brings with it a set of oceanic and atmospheric changes. Its longer duration may have brought more moderating temperatures to the North American continent as well as other regions of the world. David Rodenhuis, head of the National Weather Service's Climate Analysis Center, said that the El Niño that began in 1991 could have been a factor in the flooding of the Mississippi in 1993.[12]

A PROPHECY OF NATURE IN UPHEAVAL

Whether it's man's disturbance of the equatorial rain forests or a volcanic eruption in the Philippines, the El Niño, or a combination of the three, one thing is for certain. Nature is raising its head violently at the close of the twentieth century. Jesus spoke of these convulsions of nature prior to His return to the earth. "There will be great earthquakes, famines and pestilences in various places, and fearful events and great signs from heaven" (Luke 21:11).

The Luke 21 passage parallels Matthew 24. Both chapters describe events that will transpire prior to Christ's return. Jesus speaks primarily of what man will do to man immediately before He returns to the earth. But right in the middle of those events, He speaks of signs in nature that will point to His return. It's as though nature is reacting to the evil intents and actions of mankind.

Jesus listed in Luke 21:11 four specific eruptions of nature prior to His return: (1) great earthquakes, (2) famines, (3) pestilences, and (4) fearful and great signs from heaven. We've already seen in the previous two chapters pestilences that have crept out of the rain forests of the world, bringing with them tens of millions of deaths at the close of the millennium. But nature seems to be so unsettled that the other three signs are appearing at this late hour of history.

Earthquakes

There's nothing more descriptive of the convulsing of nature than the turmoil of an earthquake. Anyone who has felt violent tremors under foot knows how frightening it can be. People feel absolutely helpless as homes, offices, and all of the handiwork of man rock back and forth. And they are. They're completely at the mercy of nature. Jesus said that the last days would see great earthquakes. Certainly there have been earthquakes throughout history. But we live in a generation that is seeing an increasing number of earthquakes as well as the increasingly destructive power of them.

There are four basic classifications of earthquakes: tectonic, volcanic, collapse, and explosion. Tectonic is the most common type of earthquake and produces great destruction as geographic plates shift beneath the earth's surface. Volcanic earthquakes occur in conjunction with the eruption of volcanoes; such earthquakes are believed to be related to tectonic activity. Collapse earthquakes occur in underground mines and caverns.

These first three types of earthquakes were around when Jesus made that prophecy. But one is new to this generation: explosion earthquakes. These earthquakes are caused primarily by humans. "Underground nuclear explosions fired during the past several decades at a number of test sites around the world have produced substantial earthquakes," explained Bruce Bolts, professor of seismology at the University of California. "When a nuclear device is detonated . . . enormous nuclear energy is released. In millionths of a second, the pressure jumps to thousands of times the pressure of the Earth's atmosphere and the local temperature increases by millions of degrees. The surrounding rock is vaporized, creating a spherical cavity many meters in diameter."[13]

The movement of people to large cities (urbanization) and a higher density within the developing nations of the world have made people more vulnerable to an earthquake's effects.

One can't help but wonder whether such earthquakes, caused by the testing of weapons of war, has had lasting effect on the earth, and whether a relationship exists between explosion earthquakes and tectonic earthquakes.

But it's not just the drumbeat of war that has made mankind more vulnerable to earthquakes in this generation. The movement of people to large cities (urbanization) and a higher density within the developing nations of the world have made people more vulnerable to an earthquake's effects. If an earthquake strikes a dense population center, then obviously there's potential for a great amount of damage, destruction, and death. Already scientists are concerned about some of the major population centers of the world.

Consider what some reputable journals and newspapers are already saying about the risk of an earthquake to these major population centers:

Montreal and Ottawa; Boston, New York, and Charleston. "Next year, the U.S. Geological Survey expects to release new maps showing the risk of earthquakes in North America, based on seismic records of smaller quakes plus historical records of larger quakes. Preliminary findings suggest that several major urban areas—including Montreal, Ottawa, Boston, New York, and Charleston—have at least a 10 percent chance of being hit by a major earthquake within the next 50 years."[14]

Pacific Coastal Cities. "The study concludes that the Northwest coast from Vancouver Island down to northern California faces an earthquake hazard at least as great as that along the San Andreas Fault. It clearly shows that the coastal area should be considered the equivalent of San Francisco and Los Angeles."[15]

Himalayan Region of India. "A massive earthquake could hit the central Himalayan region of India at any time, geophysicists warned last week . . . which would devastate a region with a population of more than 200 million and several major dams."[16]

Los Angeles. "In two other papers in this issue, researchers warn that the L.A. Basin has probably been in an earthquake lull over the past 200 years. The calm will likely be broken by a barrage of Northridge-size earthquakes, by a single, far larger quake, or some combination of the two. . . . If the quakes were no bigger than Northridge, they must have come every 11 years on average— which would mean that Los Angeles is long overdue for a spate of Northridges."[17]

Tokyo. "A Kobe-strength earthquake in Tokyo could cripple the world's second-largest economy, send global markets into chaos and tip the USA into recession. . . . Japanese scientists say it's a question of when, not if. That's because four of the massive plates covering the earth's crust collide near Tokyo."[18]

The Kobe earthquake sent shivers throughout Japan and financial markets around the world. Japanese leaders were confident that they could handle any earthquake that might hit Japan. But when an earthquake shook the city of 1.5 million residents on January 15, 1995, many Japanese began to realize that they may not be able to outsmart nature. The Kobe quake killed almost five thousand people and caused an estimated $60 billion in losses. If a Kobe-strength quake were to hit Tokyo, experts predict global interest rates would rise "as the Japanese government borrowed billions at home and abroad to finance reconstruction," and stock indexes worldwide would dive.[19]

Economists, journalists, and politicians express such concerns should a major quake rock Tokyo. But when someone reads the words of Jesus in Matthew 24 and Luke 21, he's one step ahead of the information revolution. He's literally reading history before it happens.

Famines

Jesus said that the last days would be characterized not only by earthquakes but also by the great tragedy of famine. Again, there have been famines throughout history. But present situations produce conditions that could be more devastating than any other time in human history. By 2000 the world's population is projected to reach 6.2 billion; by A.D. 2020 more than 8 billion people will have to be fed daily. Much of the population growth will take place in the poorer nations of the world.

Obviously, that means there's potential for greater hunger and starvation than the world has previously known. Already, the United Nations "reckons that more than 700 million people in poor countries are undernourished. In 1993, 10-12 million children aged under five died from malnutrition and related illness."[20] Lester Brown, president of Worldwatch Institute in Washington D.C., believes that the world is "in the early stages of a food transition from surplus to scarcity."[21]

Much of the famine problem in the world today is produced by a combination of natural disaster and the deeds of mankind, particularly war.

One problem associated with famine is water shortage. Drought normally precedes famine. The global population has dramatically increased in the past forty-five years, causing water usage to triple. "Water tables are falling, lakes are shrinking, wetlands are disappearing, and numerous species of aquatic life are at risk of extinction . . . and people in the Middle East have heard more than one leader voice the possibility of going to war over scarce water." Scientists have deemed twenty-six countries as "water scarce nations."[22] There's enough technology today to make great strides in preventing the water problem from turning into a famine problem. But water scarcity isn't the only problem.

It's generally agreed that much of the famine problem in the world today is produced by a combination of natural disaster and the deeds of mankind, particularly war. The most obvious example in this decade is Somalia, where gruesome video pictures of babies and children with bloated stomachs have been shown to TV viewers around the world. The famine was much deeper than a prolonged drought that destroyed crops and hindered replanting. Warring factions made it impossible for the distribution of food. Human conflict caused more deaths than nature. The problem of famine is characteristic of nature reacting to man's gross sin.

Somalia's plight of war perpetuating famine is being repeated in many countries. The *New England Journal of Medicine* reported,

> In all of the countries that have reported famine so far in the 1990s—Angola, Ethiopia, Liberia, Mozambique, Somalia, and Sudan—armed conflict has been a major cause. Indeed, "food wars"—conflicts in which a principal feature has been the destruction or interdiction of civilian food supplies or of resources to produce food—became a consistent feature of the Cold War years. For example, in 1989, there were 19 such food wars. In the 1990s, armed conflicts became the dominant cause of famine worldwide.[23]

Fearful and Great Signs from Heaven

In Luke 21 Jesus described a shaking of heavenly bodies as part of the final events before His return.

> There will be signs in the sun, moon, and stars. On the earth, nations will be in anguish and perplexity at the roaring and tossing of the sea. Men will faint from terror, apprehensive of what is coming on the world, for the heavenly bodies will be shaken (verses 25–26).

Already astronomers have raised concerns about wayward heavenly bodies coming together, creating a violent upheaval. In 1994 a comet violently collided with Jupiter. Concerned space scientists saw the implications of similar future collisions in our solar system and called a meeting at the Lawrence Livermore National Laboratories in 1995 to discuss the matter. The U. S. Department of Energy, the National Aeronautics and Space Administration, and the Air Force Space Command sponsored the scientific gathering. The *San Francisco Chronicle* reported:

> 150 astronomers and space researchers from around the world meeting in Livermore urged the creation of high tech defense systems to detect threatening objects headed toward the earth and either destroy or deflect them. . . . Space scientists have long theorized about the potential danger of fast-moving celestial bodies striking Earth, but their concern was greatly heightened by the spectacular collision of the Shoemaker-Levy comet on Jupiter.[24]

Speeding asteroids and comets could "inflict far more damage on Earth than previously thought, perhaps even disrupting the climate and causing millions of deaths," the *Chronicle* reported.[25]

Already the heavenly bodies have begun to send warning signals to space scientists and astronomers. Those signals have produced so much fear and concern that they're ready to build a defense system to combat it—just what Jesus said would happen before He returned.

Nature seems to be lifting its head as the new millennium approaches. God created man to live in harmony with nature and rule over it. However, the more man goes his own way and ignores the eternal principles and truth of God's Word, then the more nature responds with violent eruptions. From the equatorial rain forests to the great urban centers of the world, nature has begun to declare the imminent return of Christ to earth. In the midst of these crises around the world, the church will be afforded the greatest opportunity in its history to bring the message of Christ to the world. The moral values of the world's people are spiraling downward even as nature seems to spin out of control. In such a setting, the church has a great opportunity, one it must approach with a renewed compassion. The world will stand helpless, needy and ready to hear the message of hope and peace in Christ.

In the gathering storm, there is a place of safety. In Part 3 we will look at the beacon and shelter against the approaching storm.

Part Three

A BEACON
IN THE STORM

During the gathering storm, human suffering will be at an all-time high. In the midst of that suffering the church will have unprecedented opportunities to minister the love of Christ. Nations will open their doors, and the gospel will go forth. Already this generation has begun to see God enable the church to take huge steps towards the fulfillment of the Great Commission, as the Iron Curtain has fallen and needy people and even governments have invited Christians to bring social and spiritual food to their hungry citizens.

Consider the opportunities already being given in the 1990s. The gospel has been preached in stadiums throughout Russia. In Mongolia, a nation that has never had Christianity, a church has been born. One evangelist (Billy Graham) in one night preached the gospel in 185 nations, and his message was translated into 116 languages. Jesus said that such things would take place before He returned.

But the Bible also warns that the Christian community will face suffering and persecution to a degree that has been unknown in church history. The Scriptures speak of a great period of tribulation in which the storm clouds of martyrdom will be felt around the globe by those who believe in Jesus. With a quick glimpse of the persecution of the church in this generation, it's not difficult to see the storm clouds on the horizon.

As the church marches forward into all the world with the gospel, its members can respond in one of two ways: with fear or faith. If we are not prepared for the storm, we will fear. If we have a strong moral and spiritual foundation, we can proceed confidently, with faith. How we live in these unique days is crucial. The gathering storm requires that our commitment to Christ and compassion for others be unswerving. Only then can we be prepared for the gathering storm.

It is likewise intimated, that, even in times of temptation, trouble, and persecution, the gospel of the kingdom shall be preached and propagated, and shall force its way through the greatest opposition. Though the enemies of the church grow very hot, and many of her friends very cool, yet the gospel shall be preached.[1]

Matthew Henry
Commenting on Matthew 24:14

And this gospel of the kingdom will be preached in the whole world as the testimony to all nations, and then the end will come.

Matthew 24:14

Chapter Seven

....

FULFILLING THE
GREAT COMMISSION

The gospel of Jesus Christ—the good news that God's Son has come to earth, lived a sinless life, and died for our sins so that we might become reconciled to God—must be preached to the uttermost parts of the earth before Jesus returns. As the storm clouds gather, it is that message that brings hope, indeed rescue to a world in upheaval. The church, responsible for bringing that message, can take heart, for the reception to the gospel has never been more positive; the opportunities never greater. What is happening in the former Iron Curtain countries is a miracle. And if it is not the fulfillment of Matthew 24:14, then it is certainly the precursor of what's about to happen—the gospel being heard in every nation.

Consider this one contrast: on Easter weekend, 1974, Fred Starkweather and I began speaking about faith in Christ with students at a Leningrad university in the Soviet Union. We asked God to lead us to someone. When we began talking to a young student from the linguistics department, he was interested and excited. "Would you tell my friends these things?" He soon returned with several of his friends, and a nearby hall began to fill with students listening as we shared the story of God's great love for mankind. For the next thirty minutes Fred and I presented the life of Christ to hungry and thirsty Russian university students. Later, as I spoke Spanish with six students, a man grabbed me by the arm

He and several colleagues brought Fred and me to an office and interrogated us for eight hours. At the end, one agent proclaimed in frustration: "By the year 2000, Christianity will no longer exist in the Soviet Union. There are only old people in the churches. By then they will have died and communism will have won a great victory over the myth."

Eighteen years later (July 1992) thousands in Norilsk, Siberia, in the former Soviet Union, listened to the gospel in the city's soccer stadium. Ironically, political prisoners and religious dissidents were forced to build the city under Stalin's cruel dictatorship. And now I had the privilege to stand in the center of the city and for the first time there proclaim the good news of God's love for mankind. Many prisoners had died for their faith while building the streets, apartments, and Norilsk's office complexes in the extreme, frigid temperatures. For me, it was an awesome moment.

I told the audience about my experience in Leningrad almost two decades earlier. I then said, "I was told by the year 2000 Christianity would not exist in the Soviet Union. Well, it's 1992, and the Soviet Union does not exist. And thousands of you have gathered here to learn about Jesus Christ." The entire crowd broke out in applause.

At that moment I realized along with thousands of Russians that something very wonderful and even miraculous had transpired. A city had been built by people who had been imprisoned there because of their faith. Now people were being sent there to tell its citizens about the faith of those who died building the city. Christianity had not only survived, but had conquered seventy years of harsh repression and persecution. A new day had dawned—one in which the gospel of Christ would travel into cities and nations that never before had an opportunity to hear about Jesus.

THE GOSPEL AND THE FALL
OF THE IRON CURTAIN

The collapse of the Soviet Union continues to produce monumental changes socially and politically for millions. The impact spiritually also has been monumental. One-third of the world's population was cut off from the public proclamation of the gospel by communist regimes. But now doors have been opened for the gospel to enter cities, communities, and even entire nations that have not had the opportunity to hear the message of God's love for man through Christ. I have watched firsthand the fulfillment of the Great Commission of Christ in previously unreachable cities and nations. After traveling in communist countries for almost twenty-five years, I now proclaim the good news of Christ in the stadiums of cities that only years earlier had no churches or Christians. I've watched churches birthed in the most remote and difficult areas of the former Soviet Union.

Observing these changes, I believe we are seeing the fulfillment of Matthew 24:14, when Jesus said that "This gospel of the kingdom will be preached in the whole world as a testimony to all nations, and then the end will come." The collapse of the Soviet Union cannot be explained by *glasnost, perestroika*, Mikhail Gorbachev, Boris Yeltsin, or any other political philosophy or personality. The collapse has occurred by the divine intervention of God in the affairs of mankind. As a result, we are now closer to the fulfillment of Christ's Great Commission and of Jesus' prophecy that once the gospel is preached everywhere, "then the end will come."

A Domino Effect

The Soviet Union's collapse has not only opened the door for the gospel in Eastern Europe, but it's had a domino effect around the world. Russia had been economically supporting socialist and communist regimes around the world. When their well of finances ran dry, many of those countries began to look elsewhere for assistance. They knew that they would have to improve their human rights records in order to get aid from the West. Consequently, many of them began to open the doors to Christian organizations. I have been able to witness firsthand the opening of several closed countries to the gospel of Christ. In all these countries, the opportunities to fulfill the Great Commission have never been greater.

In Mongolia

Although many tribal languages still have no Bible translations, Mongolia has remained for years the last country that had no Bible in its national language. The Mongolian region was known as Inner Mongolia and Outer Mongolia prior to communist rule. After the communists took over, Inner (Eastern) Mongolia became a part of China, and Outer (Western) Mongolia became an independent nation—the Republic of Mongolia. However, it was dominated primarily by the Soviet Union. Before the communists took over, mission efforts were rebuffed by the Buddhists. Once the communists took power, all religion was wiped out. An entire generation grew up without any knowledge of God.

But when the Soviet Union collapsed, the doors opened for one of the most unreached nations in the world. The nation had been void of Christianity; the masses didn't have a clue who Jesus is. After the Soviet collapse, Mongolia wanted to consider Western ideas, including faith. The young people were especially interested in learning about the West. Most of the population were young people. Therefore, *Jesus*, the highly effective evangelistic film on the life of Christ, seemed ideal. It was a "movie," and the producers, Campus Crusade for Christ, were translating it for the Mongolian people.

After conferring with me, Christian leaders asked me to go to Mongolia immediately prior to the release of *Jesus* to teach about prayer to the small band of believers. I agreed, arriving in Ulan Bator, the nation's capital, in November 1991 to meet with about seventy believers. The two groups of about thirty-five were very divided; neither had ever held any public meeting with the other. As the leaders of the two groups and I talked, we decided both groups could put their differences aside for the prayer seminars.

I sat in awe as I listened. . . . In a nation that had been void of Christianity for nearly two thousand years, God [brought] two unsuspecting Mongolians to study in communist, atheistic universities in Eastern Europe. He then sovereignly brought Christians across their paths to tell them about the Savior of the world.

The seminars went well. Not only did the church catch a vision for prayer, but also a number of non-Christians came to Christ. One day I had lunch with three of Mongolia's Christian leaders who were among the first followers of Christ. I asked them, "How did you first hear about Jesus? Your nation has never had the opportunity to hear the message of Christ. What happened in your lives to open you to the gospel?"

One told me he was a student in East Germany at the university in Leipzig when a Lutheran pastor befriended him and eventually described Christ's love. In Leipzig, "I believed on Jesus," he told me. Another attended the university in Moscow, where his roommate from Tanzania every night would pull the covers over his head before going to sleep and turn on a flashlight and begin reading a book.

"After a considerable period of time, I finally asked him about the book that he was reading. He said that it was the Bible and then began to tell me about Jesus. I didn't become a Christian then, but when I returned to Mongolia an American came through here and gave me a pamphlet. I read it and learned how to become a Christian. I gave my heart to Christ."

I sat in awe as I listened at the sovereignty and greatness of our God. In a nation that had been void of Christianity for nearly two thousand years, God orchestrated events in the lives of two unsuspecting Mongolians to study in communist, atheistic universities in Eastern Europe. He then sovereignly brought Christians across their paths to tell them about the Savior of the world. A nation void of the gospel was being prepared to receive the message of Christ. Then, at the right moment, the doors would open and Christianity for the first time in two thousand years would take hold in the hearts of the Mongolian people.

Months later I returned to Mongolia for evangelistic meetings. I preached in Ulan Bator and Darhan, a city to the north. On my first trip to Mongolia, there were no Christians in Darhan. I was thrilled to find a thriving Christian community when I returned for evangelistic meetings. At the time of this writing, there are several churches that have been established and some estimates of over two thousand believers throughout Mongolia. Jesus said, "Even so, when you see all these things, you know that it is near, right at the door" (Matthew 24:33). Part of "all these things" is the gospel going into all the world for a witness to all the nations. That's happening at this very moment.

In Albania

For many years Albania was the only official atheistic nation in the world. Here a person could receive the death penalty for any kind of belief in God. Although it shared most of its borders with Yugoslavia, Albania was more closely aligned with the Chinese communists than the Soviets. Because of its ties with the Chinese, no one really knew if the collapse of communism in Eastern Europe would affect the Albanians. Many observers thought the fall of other Eastern European communist countries would not affect Albania. After all, the country did not depend on the Soviet economy as its neighbors did. But the 1990s was God's moment for Albania to receive the gospel.

In April 1994, I stood in the center of the Albanian towns of Burrel and Lezhe and proclaimed the gospel to most of the towns' inhabitants. I was overwhelmed as I recalled the country's origins. During the late 1980s, while I participated at a pastors conference for Baptist leaders in Brazil, a woman studying about Albania led the pastors and myself in prayer for Albania. She described the persecution in the country, including the fact that people could receive the death penalty for any belief in God. She concluded by asking the pastors, "Please, would you pray for Albania? Pray that God would open the doors for the gospel in Albania." Those pastors fell to their knees and began to cry out for God to open Albania to the gospel.

Several years later, here I was, invited to conduct the evangelistic meetings by Brazilian Baptist missionaries! Brazilian Baptist leaders prayed for that day. God not only answered their prayers, but also sent some of them to the nation. It was my second trip into Albania and such a thrill to see scores of churches and thousands of believers throughout the nation.

During my first trip to the nation in 1993 there was also a very moving moment. I was asked by a longtime friend,

Charlie Cutts, to come to Albazan, the Albanian city where he had started a church. Charlie introduced me by saying that I could identify with the hurts and sorrows that the Albanian people had experienced. He told them that I had been arrested three times for preaching the gospel. I then stood and preached to the people.

Following my message, an old man came up, threw his arms around me, and began weeping and kissing my neck and cheeks. He sobbed and sobbed. After he gained his composure, we sat down together and he told me his story. He had been a professor at the university in Tirana. He believed that God existed. He began sharing his views with some of the students. When the government discovered his views, he was immediately thrown in prison. Other believers were also in prison. Few lived to see the day in which Christ could be proclaimed publicly in the nation.

The old man told me, "When the pastor said that you had been arrested three times, I was overwhelmed. I didn't know that there was anyone who could identify with what I have been through. I didn't know if there was anyone who could understand how wonderful this day is."

To be honest, I couldn't fully appreciate what the old man felt and had experienced. He had gone through things too horrible to even speak. But I understood a little of the joy and wonder that he felt over "this day." It's really difficult for many people to appreciate and understand how wonderful "this day" really is. For those of us who have prayed, worked, and struggled to bring the gospel to communist countries for a quarter of a century, it's a miracle. If this isn't the fulfillment of Matthew 24:14, then it is certainly a preview of what is about to happen.

The Uttermost Parts of the Earth

Some may protest, saying, "Wait a minute. Jesus said that the gospel would go into all the world. Places like

China, Cuba, and the Muslim countries still are closed to the gospel." As one who has traveled and ministered extensively in the "difficult" areas of the world, I must disagree. The doors to some of these areas of the world may not be opened in the same manner as in the Soviet Union, but God is working mightily in many of those regions.

Missionaries told of thousands gathering in the desert of one Islamic nation. . . . [Later the missionaries] produced for me pictures of thousands of people meeting secretly in the desert in one of the most closed Muslim countries in the world.

For instance, during three visits to *Cuba* during 1994–95, I found tremendous growth in the churches. At most evangelistic meetings in several churches there were as many people standing outside the churches to hear the message as were inside. Between my visits, the churches grew rapidly. At one church, for instance, I found a people excited about Christ during my first preaching visit. When I returned a few months later, church leaders had cut a rectangular hole in the wall immediately behind the pulpit. Entering the auditorium, I thought the people behind the opening were reflections in a large mirror; I soon realized that that they were in a room behind the pulpit, just as packed as the auditorium. The church had practically doubled in just a few months.

Significant growth also is underway in the Christian church in *China* and also *the Muslim world*. Because of the nature of the danger to Christians in those countries, I can't be specific about what is happening at this time. But God is working mightily in those countries. Tremendous church growth is taking place in China, in spite of many obstacles. There are verbal reports of entire villages that have been converted to Christ. The gospel continues to go forward in that great nation where one-sixth of the world's population lives.

Meanwhile, underground churches have begun in some of the most closed Muslim countries. At one international prayer conference, missionaries told of thousands gathering in the desert of one Islamic nation. Being a skeptic, I privately questioned some of the leaders about those claims. They produced for me pictures of thousands of people meeting secretly in the desert in one of the most closed Muslim countries in the world. They told how they never met in the same place twice. Despite the difficulties encountered in those countries, God is sovereign and is bringing His word to pass in these last days.

Numerous mission agencies and Christian denominations are now targeting the more difficult areas of the world, demonstrating a renewed concern for fulfilling the Great Commission of Christ. Efforts have been doubled and a new sense of cooperation seems to exist between church and mission agencies, as they recognize the recent opening for the gospel.

For instance, Campus Crusade for Christ and Southern Baptists recently teamed up to bring the gospel to the countless unreached villages in *Albania*. Teams were ferried by helicopter into remote villages, and colleagues have reported great success in the cooperative effort. Numerous mission agencies also have worked together in the CoMission effort to evangelize *Russia*. There also is great cooperation to present the gospel throughout Eastern Europe. In addition, I am presently serving on a committee with leaders of several major organizations who are planning strategy to attempt to bring the gospel to every person and people group in this generation. Clearly there is a global vision underway.

What was once unthinkable is quickly becoming reality. I believe this generation has the actual potential to fulfill the words of Christ, "and the gospel of the kingdom will go into all the world for a witness to the nations, and then the end shall come."

GLOBAL TECHNOLOGY AND THE GREAT COMMISSION

But there's one last evidence that the Christian church stands on the threshold of fulfilling the Great Commission. Modern technology has made it possible to bring the message of Christ where missionaries and mission agencies can't go. Billy Graham's "Global Mission" brought the message of Christ to 185 nations and 10 million people and was translated into 116 languages. Though the live event occurred in Puerto Rico, the gospel beamed by live satellite transmission and delayed videotape was broadcast to countries as far away as Egypt and Nepal. In Egypt, a reported 9,000 people in this largely Islamic nation responded to Graham's invitation.[2] In Nepal 25,000 people gathered in the stadium in Katmandu to hear the great Christian evangelist proclaim over satellite the gospel of Jesus Christ, according to one Nepalese leader. That's remarkable considering that for many years the country has been a Hindu kingdom. In fact, Christians in the 1980s were being thrown in prison for evangelizing the Nepalese.

Satellites now beam radio and television messages around the globe. Many in the broadcast industry are saying satellite radio is the superhighway of Christian broadcasting. With this new technology, broadcasts can be received over a large region of the world via a satellite dish in the listener's home.

In this latest broadcast specialty, the Europeans are ahead of North Americans. Our ministry, God's Love in Action, began broadcasting on a British-based Christian satellite network in 1995. The broadcast has the potential to be picked up via satellite dish and/or through cable in 50 million homes in Europe and northern Africa.[3] Such broadcast innovations are appealing to churches in the East as well. Friends in India have asked our ministry to produce some evangelistic television programs to be beamed from India via satellite throughout the entire Asian region. The broadcast would go into such countries as China, India, Tibet, Nepal, North Korea, Vietnam, Cambodia, Iran, Iraq, and Saudi Arabia.

Politically and technically, new capabilities make the worldwide declaration of the gospel possible and even probable. And spiritually a hunger exists. Thus the church has an opportunity to complete that task that Jesus gave to His disciples before ascending to heaven. We are the generation that is seeing the gospel go into all the world before the end comes. And Jesus said, "Even so, when you see all these things, you know that it is near, right at the door" (Matthew 24:33).

I have always envied those Christians who all through church history were martyred for Christ Jesus our Lord. What a privilege to live for our Lord and to die for Him as well.[1]

Mehdi Dibaj
Letter to his family two years
before he was murdered for his faith

But before all this, they will lay hands on you and persecute you. They will deliver you to synagogues and prisons, and you will be brought before kings and governors, and all on account of my name. This will result in your being witnesses to them. But make up your mind not to worry beforehand how you will defend yourselves. For I will give you words and wisdom that none of your adversaries will be able to resist or contradict. You will be betrayed even by parents, brothers, relatives, and friends, and they will put some of you to death. All men will hate you because of me.

Jesus (Luke 21:12–17)
describing events before He returned to the earth

Chapter Eight

....

THE GREAT PERSECUTION

During June 1994, I stood in a stadium in Chernauts, Ukraine, to proclaim the gospel of Jesus. Though I had preached in similar stadiums throughout the former Soviet Union during the previous four years, this was the first time I told the complete story of my arrest in Leningrad for telling college students about Christ. It was a time of persecution, I said, but also a time when God gave me the power to forgive those who had arrested me.

During the final Sunday of the Chernauts meetings, my wife and I had lunch with some of the Christian leaders, including the bishop of the official Baptist and Evangelical Church Council. His wife surprised us as she began to weep. She had been through her own persecution as a child growing up.

"When you told of having been arrested for telling others about Christ, something happened in my heart," she said. "It was as though God began to apply medicine to my wounded soul."

"Why do you say that?" I asked.

She told us that when she was only eleven, her parents were arrested because of their faith. "They did no harm to anyone, but simply tried to live in peace with God and their fellow man. One day they were arrested and sent away to prison in Siberia," she explained.

"I was taken and placed on a train to a mountain region. I didn't know anyone there. I was left an orphan, a street child. But God was faithful. A woman from the Orthodox church found me at the train station. She introduced herself to me and asked me where I was staying.

"I told her that I didn't know anyone there and related what had happened to me and my family. She asked me to come home with her. I did and I lived with her until I was twenty-two years old. I then returned to the Ukraine. My mother was released from prison, and I saw her again for the first time in over ten years.

"My father died while in prison in Siberia," she continued. "I never saw him again.

"Because of all I had gone through as a child, my heart has been very, very sick. But when you told about your arrest, something happened inside. I felt like God touched my heart and began a real healing of the hurt that has been there for such a long time."

PERSECUTION: TRAGEDY AND TRIUMPH

When she had finished the story, everyone at the table sat in silence, overwhelmed with the tragedy and triumph in her life. She is among scores of people I've met who have suffered great persecution and deep hurt because of their faith. An entire book could be filled with their stories. Their only crime was their faith in Christ and their willingness to express that faith to others. As evangelical Christianity offers a solution to the gathering storm, and as Christians stand for biblical moral values, political and spiritual opposition will increase. The price for proclaiming the gospel has been and will continue to be high. Whether in communist countries, Islamic nations, the secular West, or revolutionary forces in poorer countries, Christians face increasing persecution.

Some of the greatest persecution has occurred and continues to occur in former communist countries. We will look at several countries and see a pattern that Jesus said would continue in the last days.

TALES FROM ROMANIA

Nick Gheorghita was one of the foremost medical doctors in Romania and an outstanding Christian layman when members of the Second Baptist Church of Oradea called him to become their pastor. Dr. Nick accepted the call, but the securitate (Romania's dreaded secret police) didn't want a man of his intellect and abilities in that position. So they refused to permit him to live in Oradea. I recall visiting secretly with Dr. Nick during those days. He had to sleep in a different home every night so that he wouldn't be found by the secret police. A man of great intellect and compassion—a man who had so much to offer society—was hunted like an animal. The only reason for such treatment was that he was trying to obey God and help His people. Today Dr. Nick is a man of deep faith and serves as the executive secretary of the Baptist Union in Romania.

During the height of persecution in communist-dominated Eastern Europe, values were completely inverted. Right was wrong and wrong became right.

Romanian Peter Dugalescu faced similar treatment when he was called to be pastor of the First Baptist Church of Timisoara. One night Peter showed me the scars in his body where the securitate attempted to kill him. His only crime was trying to effectively pastor the people in his church. After the Romanian revolution, Peter was elected to the national parliament and serves there today. Many others faced the same kind of persecution. It's important to note that these weren't fanatical people who had martyr complexes such as some of the false messiahs mentioned in chapter 2. These were solid Christians and good citizens in their countries who are recognized internationally today for their service to their communities and their churches.

During the height of persecution in communist-dominated Eastern Europe, values were completely inverted. Right was wrong and wrong became right. Those who wanted to do good were treated as criminals, while their persecutors actually believed that they were doing a service to society by eliminating such people. Jesus told His disciples that such a day would come. "In fact," He said, "a time is coming when anyone who kills you will think he is offering a service to God" (John 16:2).

The apostle John also wrote of a time of great persecution immediately before the return of Christ. During this period of great persecution, a massive martyrdom of God's people will occur (Revelation 6:9–11). I don't think that we are necessarily seeing the fulfillment of that prophecy at this moment. But there continues to be growing persecution of Christians and anti-Christian sentiment in many regions of the world. The storm clouds are already gathering.

PERSECUTION AFTER THE
COLLAPSE OF COMMUNISM

Many people think that persecution completely ceased in Eastern Europe and the former Soviet Union after the collapse of communism. Not true.

In *Macedonia,* a former Yugoslavian republic, police warned me in November 1995 to not speak publicly about Christ. As I sat in the office of the leading police officials in Ohrid, a city that borders Albania, authorities cited an old law written by the communists to keep people from preaching publicly about Christ. Although officials claimed that Macedonia was a democracy and U.S. troops were patrolling its borders at the time, they were quite antagonistic to believers. Evangelical Christians there are a small minority of the population. Already they are beginning to experience difficulties similar to those they experienced under communist rulers in Yugoslavia.

As noted earlier, *Albania* for many years could give the death penalty to any person who professed belief in God. Since freedom has come to that part of the world, the gospel has gone forward in the nation, and by the end of 1995 an estimated four thousand citizens were evangelical Christians. But already some government officials are beginning to beat the drum of persecution. Evangelical Christians in the nation were shocked when Sokol Miraka, director of religious affairs under the Council of Ministers, was quoted in an article in the independent daily Tirana newspaper *Koha Jone,* saying, "Under names such as Evangelical, Baptist, etc., these sects—which have come from the four corners of the globe —could be hiding centers or perpetrators of terrorist activities, spy operations, or any other kind of subversive behaviour."[2] His comments sounded very similar to political propaganda against the Tutsi peoples in Rwanda right before the genocide in 1994.

In *the former Soviet Union*, official government persecution may be past; yet the farther one goes from the center (Moscow), the worse conditions become for believers. In 1993 evangelical Christians invited me to lead citywide evangelistic meetings in Komsomolsk, Siberia. Komsomolsk was named after the communist youth league and was a strong center for communism. In 1993 communists still controlled the major political positions in the city.

When I arrived in the city, I found that our posters advertising the meetings had printed notices placed over them. The notices attacked my character, very unusual since no one in the city had ever met me. I was accused of coming to the city to get money out of the people and spread propaganda about America. Of course, we never take any offerings in our meetings. Rather, our ministry pays for all of the expenses of the meetings. And my message is always a simple one of God's love for sinful mankind.

Thirty members of First Baptist Church, Longview, Texas, accompanied me to minister to the Komsomolsk people. Their pastor, Kenneth Hall, and I walked that first evening to the House of Culture where the meetings were and we were amazed to see full-uniform Kazakhs standing guard at the entrances. They were carrying whips and challenging anyone who wanted to come into the meetings. Police were also there, but did nothing to stop the Kazakh soldiers. Christians in the city were heartbroken. They thought they had freedom. But now they were being prevented from presenting Christ to their city.

Of course, few people were willing to attempt to enter the meetings when they faced soldiers with whips. But some did come and they placed their faith in Christ.

On the final Sunday, the local pastor asked Dr. Hall to assist him in an open-air baptismal service. Ken baptized and I preached outside at the beach, where the new Christians were baptized . In spite of the obstacles, this was a tremendous opportunity to preach to hundreds of non-Christians. I invited everyone to come with us to the House of Culture. Now hundreds came. The Kazakhs were taken totally by surprise and the House of Culture was filled with people hungry for God.

I preached and many gave their hearts to Christ. It was exciting to see such response to the gospel. The local newspaper admitted we had done a good work in the city, then protested that when we were gone, the new Christians would be left without any help. What the newspaper didn't know was that we had an agreement with the local Baptist church to send two Eastern European Bible college students to live there for one year to assist the new believers.

The two young men eventually came . . . planning to stay at the Baptist church facilities. But the day they arrived someone burned the church to the ground.

The two young men eventually came to Komsomolsk, planning to stay at the Baptist church facilities. But the day they arrived someone burned the church to the ground. There's still anti-Christian fervor in many parts of the former Soviet Union. Latent hatred of Christianity resides in many areas of the Commonwealth of Independent States. For years, many Siberian newspapers reported that Baptists and Pentecostals offered their children as human sacrifices. Such prejudice won't be easily overcome. In fact, if economic conditions don't improve in Russia and the former republics, there could be an even more severe persecution than known previously. This would be especially true if a strong dictator emerges.

WORLDWIDE PERSECUTION

Outside the West, tremendous church growth is occurring worldwide. The gospel is making inroads into regions of the world that have previously been closed to Christians.

At the same time, there's a gathering storm of persecution. It's costing Christians around the world to be followers of Christ. There's never been a time in church history when Christians have suffered as greatly as during this generation.

Some of the greatest human rights abuses this century have taken place against the Christian church, and yet for the most part they've gone unreported by the major news outlets. As I've traveled internationally, I continually run across tragic stories of persecution. In Indonesia, one Christian woman described how her teenaged son, enroute to a youth meeting at their church, was kidnapped by a Muslim family who wanted that young man to marry their daughter. They brought him to an area of Indonesia that was totally Muslim and forced him to marry the Muslim girl. After two weeks of being held hostage, he found a way to escape and made his way back home.

But it was too dangerous for him to stay in Indonesia. His parents had to send him to Australia to live. He may have been killed if he had stayed in Indonesia.

A young leader continually gave pleas for help for his Christian brothers and sisters in Nigeria. Muslims have burned and destroyed the homes of Christian leaders in the northern part of the country where a Muslim majority dominates. At "Singapore 87," an international congress for emerging, younger Christian world leaders, he pleaded for Christians in the West to help through prayer. In many Muslim countries, people receive the death penalty for coming to personal faith in Christ. At the Singapore congress I met Christian leaders from around the world who faced extremely difficult situations in their homelands.

It's not just Christians in Muslim and Eastern European countries who are facing persecution. People in the West who follow the Bible as their true source of authority and values in life are beginning to have to pay the price for following Christ, suffering ridicule and discrimination and even loss of job or advancement because of their beliefs. In a day when sin is no longer called sin, when the news media and government officials relabel sodomy and homosexuality as "an alternative lifestyle," Christians find themselves recast as intolerant and divisive and subject to increasing scrutiny for their beliefs.

In his classic *1984*, George Orwell described a society in which the language would be changed. New terms and new meaning to the language would be formulated to impose a new philosophy and value system upon society. Orwell appears to have been correct about what would happen, only incorrect about when it would happen. The book perhaps could have been more accurately titled *1994 and Beyond*.

Today the word *sin* is being banished from the vocabulary of most Americans, and a person can be called insensitive or even bigoted for calling certain activities sinful. In fact, sensitivity training has invaded corporate America, with "diversity seminars" warning workers to embrace homosexual coworkers and accept feminist positions.

In 1995, for example, AT&T conducted diversity training at its offices to teach its workers to rethink their attitudes towards homosexuality. Several questions seemed to imply heterosexuality was only an option, not a normal form of sexual expression, as society has believed during most of the twentieth century. Some of the questions were as follows: 1. What do you think causes heterosexuality? 2. If one has never had a same sex lover, is it possible that heterosexuality can be overcome with the help of a good gay relationship? 3. Why do many heterosexuals feel compelled to seduce others into their lifestyle? 4. Knowing that 99% of reported rapists and 98% of child molesters are heterosexuals, do you consider it safe to expose children to heterosexual teachers, coaches, counsellors, and scout leaders?[3]

Such questions are being used by other major corporations as well in an attempt to redefine moral values. In news reports and corporate activities, attempts are being made to cast a homosexual lifestyle as normal; this inversion of morality is growing in the West. Some U.S. city governments and even the family theme park Disney World have extended insurance benefits to the live-in partners of homosexual employees. When the Florida State Baptist Convention protested a decision of the Walt Disney Company to allow homosexual and lesbian theme nights at its parks, a company spokesman said Disney regretted that the Baptists have "chosen to take that position," saying the theme park is open to all members of the community.[4]

As pluralism grows, so does the rejection of those who believe in absolute moral values within Western civilization. Anyone who holds to the absolute values communicated in the Scriptures quickly becomes the odd person and is dubbed a part of the "fanatical religious right."

For Christians, there seems to be a higher price tag for proclaiming the gospel and upholding God's standards. Such persecution suggests that the world is moving rapidly in a direction of a "great tribulation period" as described in Revelation 6–9. When the first seal is opened in Revelation 6:1–2, John gives indications of a great storm that humanity will face. As John Walvoord, Bible scholar and chancellor of Dallas Theological Seminary, wrote about those verses,

> As the first seal is opened, John in his vision hears the noise of thunder, a symbolic token of a coming storm. On a warm summer day one can hear thunder in the distance even though the sun is still shining where he is. The approaching dark clouds and the roar of the thunder presage the beginning of the storm.[5]

THE SIGN OF THE MARTYRS

That storm is rapidly approaching. I don't believe that we're in the midst of the storm, but signs of its approach are here. One of the devastating effects of that storm is the martyrdom of Christians (Revelation 6:9–11). The increase in the number of martyrs at the end of this millennium makes me conclude that the great tribulation storm is not far away.

At the Lausanne II Congress on World Evangelization in 1989, Christian leaders heard reports of the great things that God is doing in our world as the millennium comes to an end. However, they also read some startling statistics in the "Quick-Reference Global Statistical Index" contained in the congress notebook.

One of every four people who have been martyred for Christ in all of history has died during this generation.

There researchers David Barrett and Frank Jansen posted totals for martyrs through church history. From A.D. 33 until 1989 they calculated that 40.4 million followers of Christ died for their beliefs. Significantly, the number since 1900 was 26.6 million, or almost 66 percent of the total. Thus two of every three Christians who have died a martyr's death did so this century. But that doesn't tell the whole story. More than 37 percent, almost 10 million (a total of 9,965,000), were martyred between 1950 and 1989.[6] That means one of every four people who have been martyred for Christ in all of history has died during this generation.

According to Barrett, one-third of all martyrs today are women. He estimates that 52,000 women died serving Christ in 1994. As professor of missiometrics at Regent

University in Virginia, he estimated that about five hundred Christians died for Christ in A.D. 100. But his research shows that 156,000 Christians were martyred in 1994. "One in every 200 Christians can expect to be martyred in his or her lifetime," Barrett says, and claims that Christians in the West only know "the tip of the iceberg" about martyrdom.[7]

The church has suffered globally more in this generation than in any other era of history. I know that may be difficult to grasp, especially for Western Christians who worship regularly in air-conditioned sanctuaries with comfortable pews, and look out stained-glass windows. But the reality of the Christian world is great suffering for the followers of Christ. For most Christians around the world it costs a great deal to follow Jesus—in many cases their very own lives. They have no difficulty seeing the storm clouds on the horizon. Much of the Christian world is already experiencing unprecedented discrimination, and such suffering has begun to come to Western Christians. They too incur the wrath of a world system opposed to Christ and His teaching.

It's time to look up and see the storm clouds gathering; and it's time to realize as the church of Jesus Christ that we can stand strong during such persecution and model the peace that only He can give.

Thus, as Christ is the Center, Source, and Goal of the universe, His cross is the center, source and goal of reconciliation. . . . By the way of that cross I am reconciled to God, and through it I find rest, infinite, eternal, undying. At last my rest shall be rest with the whole creation, for the cosmic order will be restored through the mystery of God's suffering as revealed in the cross.[1]

G. Campbell Morgan
The Bible and the Cross

"Why do you call me, 'Lord, Lord,' and do not do what I say? I will show you what he is like who comes to me and hears my words and puts them into practice. He is like a man building a house who dug down deep and laid the foundation on rock. When a flood came, the torrent struck that house but could not shake it, because it was well built. But the one who hears my words and does not put them into practice is like a man who built a house on the ground without a foundation. The moment the torrent struck that house, it collapsed and its destruction was complete."

Luke 6:46–49

Chapter Nine

....

THE ONLY
SAFE PLACE

In Part 3 I have suggested the only rescue from the gathering storm can be found among the people of the church; they have the message. Yet I must caution that the answer is not the institution called *church* nor the people who follow Christ (though they are powerful influences for God's glory when they obey His leading).

As we see the fire of God's judgment on the horizon of human history, there's only one safe place to stand: where the fire of God's judgment has already passed. Two thousand years ago, the fire of God's judgment burned as no other time in history. On a hill outside Jerusalem, the only sinless human to ever walk upon the face of the earth hung on a cross between two common criminals. His death was a sacrifice for mankind's sins, and made available forgiveness from God. He became the way every person, Jew and Gentile, male and female, could satisfy the judgment of God's righteous wrath.

This Jewish rabbi was all God and yet all man. He was the God-man Jesus. Luke referred to Him as the Son of Man, while John called Him the Son of God. Jesus' life was totally pure; indeed He was purity itself. Jesus lived and loved as no other man had ever lived or loved—without sin. Jesus was called *Immanuel*, which means "God with us" (Matthew 1:23).

Jesus was born with one purpose—to die. All men will die, but Jesus was born to die. Because God is holy and all people are sinful, humanity stands condemned and hopeless. Evil could not go unpunished. Otherwise mankind would have destroyed itself long ago. Therefore, Jesus came to the earth, conceived of the Spirit of God and born of a virgin woman; thus He was all God and all man. He lived in perfect harmony with the heavenly Father who created the universe. Then He gave Himself to die—to take the punishment for the sins of mankind.

All men will die, but Jesus was born to die. . . .
God, in His infinite love . . . decided to give of
His very own self—His own Son to bring
people back to Himself.

Some think that Roman soldiers or Jewish religious leaders killed Jesus. No, Jesus Himself said He could have chosen to call ten legions of angels to take Him off the cross. But He didn't, knowing that He must fulfill the Scriptures by dying for people's sins (Matthew 26:53–54). As a man who lived without sinning, He was the only person capable of taking the punishment for man's sin. All others deserved to be punished. He did not and so became a sacrifice, the perfect substitution for your and my sins.

As Jesus hung on the cross, He looked towards heaven and, in His humanity, cried out, "My God, my God, why have You forsaken me?" (Matthew 27:46). At that moment the sinless man bore all the wrath and judgment of an absolutely holy God. The Father turned His back on the Son as the fire of God's judgment burned with fury on that hill outside Jerusalem. Jesus took the punishment for the sins of all who would believe on Him and receive Him into their lives. Such love the world has never before or since seen.

Yes, the only safe place to stand during these last days is where the fire of God's judgment has already been, at the cross outside Jerusalem two thousand years ago. As we place our faith in Him and His act on that cross to redeem us, we place our feet on holy ground. It's the place where the love of God and the wrath of God collided. The wrath of God was poured out on the Son of God as He took the punishment for our sins, and the love of God was poured out for sinful mankind. God forgave our sins by Jesus' sacrificial death. There the judgment for our sins has been satisfied. We need to receive that gift by turning to Christ.

Many people may respond by saying, "I believe in Jesus, but I'm still unsure about my eternal destiny. I look around at the rapidly changing world, and it frightens me. I'm not prepared for the coming of Christ. How can I know for sure that my feet have been planted on that secure ground? How can I know that I'm in that safe place?"

We can only be prepared for the second coming of Christ when we know Him in the power of His first coming.

A person must settle two great heart issues in order to know that he is living in that place of safety and security during these unique and historic days. The first is the issue of the repentant heart and the second is that of a believing heart. We can only be prepared for the second coming of Christ when we know Him in the power of His first coming.

A REPENTANT HEART

When Jesus came the first time, John the Baptist went before Him. He prepared the way for the advent of the Savior of the world. His message was simple, "Repent, for the kingdom of heaven is at hand." It was the message of repentance that prepared people for the first coming of Christ. And I believe that same message of repentance will prepare us for the second coming of Christ.

After the genocide passed that had ravaged Rwanda, I was asked one evening to address many of the government leaders. I spoke on the necessity of forgiveness in order for the healing of hearts to take place in the country. One of the cabinet ministers responded to my message, and his words were wise, reflecting the biblical principle of repentance. "The international community has placed a lot of pressure on us to give amnesty to those who fled the country. Many of them participated in the genocide. Of course, those who had nothing to do with the genocide have nothing to fear. They are welcome to return and do not need amnesty. They can live here in peace and already many have returned."

He then said very firmly, "We are prepared to issue amnesty. But that amnesty is conditional. There must be an acknowledgment and repentance of the deeds that were done by those that committed the atrocities, or there can be no amnesty. Many of those who committed the atrocities have never even acknowledged what they did. It would then be suicidal for us to issue amnesty to them. They would simply return to the country, and within a matter of time we would have another genocide in Rwanda. If they have had no change of heart about what they did, then it would be foolish to let them back into the nation."

I thought deeply about what the official said. I knew that Rwanda could probably not survive as a nation if there was another genocide. The official was right. Even though the government was ready to make a provision for amnesty, there still had to be repentance on the part of those who committed the atrocities. As he spoke, I realized how relevant what he said was to the Christian faith. We can't say that we accept God's eternal amnesty and at the same time refuse to acknowledge that we've wronged Him. It's impossible to accept His amnesty or absolute forgiveness and at the same time say to Him, "I'll continue to live the way I want to live. I'll lie. I'll cheat. I'll continue to shake my fist in Your face. I'll do what I want to do. You must give me amnesty, but I'll continue to live in rebellion against You and all that is in Your kingdom."

Only a repentant heart can come to Christ and receive His grace and forgiveness. But what is repentance? It's a biblical word that simply means a change of heart—a change of direction. Imagine a man who's driving his car in a northerly direction on a highway, slowing his car as he sees someone seeking a ride. As he looks closer, he can't believe his eyes. It's Jesus, the Son of God. "Jesus, You shouldn't be stranded on the highway," the driver says, as he stops the car. "Please, get into my car. I'll give You a ride."

But Jesus does something very unusual. He doesn't get in the passenger's side of the car. He comes around to the driver's side and says, "Move over." He then takes over the steering wheel and turns the automobile around to head south. He begins to drive the opposite direction.

That's a picture of repentance. It's allowing Christ to take control of the steering wheel of our lives. It's a recognition that we've been going the wrong direction in life and a willingness to allow Him to turn our lives around and head in the opposite direction. Jesus once spoke of pending judgment and said:

I tell you, no! But unless you repent, you too will all perish. Or those eighteen who died when the tower in Siloam fell on them—do you think they were more guilty than all the others living in Jerusalem? I tell you, no! But unless you repent, you too will all perish. (Luke 13:3–5)

If we are to be prepared for the coming judgment, we must have a repentant heart. There must be a change of heart and a change of direction in our lives.

A BELIEVING HEART

While *repentance* is a willingness to forsake the direction of life that we have taken, *faith* is an assurance that Christ is sufficient to forgive us, transform our lives, and keep us safe in the day of judgment. It's much more than just believing the right things intellectually. It's more than emotionally desiring Christ in our lives. After all, even the Devil believes the right things. As the apostle James wrote, "You believe that there is one God. Good! Even the demons believe that—and shudder" (James 2:19). Satan has an intellectual faith: He knows the facts about the life, death, and resurrection of Christ. But that is not a faith that saves from judgment.

In 1995, I explained the nature of faith to thousands of Brazilians in a stadium near the Amazon River by placing a chair at the front of the stage. "How many of you believe that this chair will hold me up?" I asked. Everyone responded positively. I then asked, "But is the chair holding me up? Of course not. I believe intellectually that it will hold me up. But it's not holding me up. That's not genuine faith."

"I'm really tired," I told the audience. "I want the chair to hold me up. But it's still not holding me up. I believe mentally that it can, and I emotionally want it to hold me up, but it's not doing it. What will it take for this chair to hold me up?" I then sat down in the chair and said, "Now, that's faith."

Faith is believing intellectually that Jesus is God come in human flesh. It's believing that He died for our sins, was buried, and arose from the grave on the third day. All of that is a part of faith, but not faith itself. Faith is sensing a felt need for Christ. It's desiring Him and His forgiveness and power to change our lives. Faith contains both elements of the intellect and emotions. But faith also has a third component. It's volitional. It's a choice. It's understanding who Jesus is and recognizing our need of Him. We must then make a choice to entrust our lives to Him. When we make that decision He becomes the place of safety in the midst of all the storms of life.

Jesus spoke a parable about two men who built homes (Matthew 7:24–27). One built his home on a foundation of sand, while the other built his on a solid rock foundation. When a storm came, the house resting on the sandy foundation collapsed, but the house built on the rock withstood the storm. Jesus then compared those two men's efforts to those of most people. His parable remains relevant two thousand years later. As the storm swiftly approaches, and brings with it the threat of a flood from rising waters, only those who have a firm foundation of repentance and faith will be able to stand in the midst.

Sensing the Urgency

The tempo of change has sped up in recent years, and many sense an urgency to have their lives firmly planted. Jesus is the Rock of our salvation who can stabilize our lives. Today is the day and now is the acceptable time to allow Christ to keep us safe in the midst of the storm. It's quickly advancing.

I placed my personal faith in Christ as a student at Louisiana State University. Only a few months after I made that decision, I heard a man recount a dramatic event in his life. Late one night he was driving across a causeway over Lake Pontchartrain in my home state of Louisiana. Pontchartrain Causeway is one of the world's longest highways over water. As he was driving on a lonely, desolate part of that span, he saw a man in the middle of the bridge. The man had removed his jacket and was frantically waving it and yelling, "Stop! Stop! Stop!" The driver didn't know what to do. *This guy could be a crazy man or a thief,* he told himself. *But he could be someone who really needs help.* My friend began asking himself questions, *Should I stop? Should I keep going? What should I do?*

He finally decided to stop the car and see if the man needed help. The man came running up to the car as the driver rolled down his window. The man began shouting, almost out of breath: "I'm so glad you stopped. There's been a terrible tragedy. A part of the bridge has been knocked out. If you had continued going, you would have gone into the lake and drowned."

The driver got out of his car, hugged the man, and then took off his own coat. He too stood in the middle of the bridge and began waving his coat and yelling to others, "Stop! Stop! Stop!"

That story vividly describes what happened in my life as a university student. I was headed down a highway in life. I was going my own way close to the midnight hour of history. God was the furthest thought from my mind. I was living for one person—myself. One night I encountered a man in the middle of the highway of life yelling, "Stop! Stop! Stop living the way you're living. Turn your life to Christ. Place your faith in Him."

That night I made a decision, the most important decision I've ever made. I decided to stop living my own way and to place my faith in Christ. He came into my life and completely changed me. He forgave me all the wrongs in my life. He gave me a foundation in life that has enabled me to live victoriously in the worst of storms. I found purpose and meaning in life. Since then I've been traveling the highways of the world and telling others, "Stop! Stop going the way you're going! There's a great tragedy awaiting you on this highway. Turn now! There's a place of safety. Place your faith in Christ."

> *"There's a great tragedy awaiting you on this highway. Turn now! There's a place of safety . . . in Christ."*

How urgent is the need to respond to Christ's offer? I am not breathless nor fanatical, but I am sure of the need. So I say: "The hour is late in human history. The storm is approaching. Christ is coming. Are you prepared?"

Books have a way of traveling highways upon which I could never journey. It may be that this book has found its way into the bedroom of your home. Or maybe it's traveling with you on an airplane or has become a companion to you in a lonely motel room. But the message is loud and clear. You have a decision to make. It's a simple choice—heaven or hell; life or death; to trust in Christ or to trust in yourself. No one can make that decision for you—no friend, family member, pastor, priest, or rabbi. You have to make it.

If you would like to make that decision, then let me offer you a prayer that may be helpful to you. The words aren't as important as the attitude of your heart. If this prayer expresses what's in your heart, why don't you just whisper it to God right now.

Dear God, I know that I've failed You. I've been living for myself, and I know that's wrong. I'm not prepared for the approaching storm, for the day when I have to face You. I ask You to forgive me. I turn from my sinful ways and place my faith in Your Son, Jesus. I open my heart and life to Jesus. I believe in You, Jesus. Come and live in me.

Thank You for hearing my prayer and answering it. I love You. In Jesus' name I ask these things. Amen.

If you sincerely prayed that prayer and meant what you prayed, you can be assured that you've placed your feet on the solid Rock of Christ's salvation.[2] You need now to begin to live for Him. As you stand in the place of safety, you can begin to reach out to others and help them find that place of safety.

"Where was the church?"
Deogratius Kayumba
Chancellor, National University of Rwanda
Asked after the genocide of 1994

....

*Do not conform any longer to the pattern of this world,
but be transformed by the renewing of your mind. Then you
will be able to test and approve what God's will is—his good,
pleasing and perfect will.*
Romans 12:2

Chapter Ten

....

THE TRANSFORMED CHRISTIAN

When I speak, I always try to discern the spiritual atmosphere and the level of receptivity of the audience. This night, on a scale of one to ten, I felt the level of receptivity was minus five as I began to address a dinner gathering of professors and the chancellor of the National University of Rwanda. Student leaders who had responded to the gospel and placed their faith in Christ were hosting the dinner because of their concern for their professors' spiritual welfare.

The evening was thick with tension. Only one year earlier the 1994 genocide had devastated the nation; now a time of healing was underway, and I had been invited to speak to the masses, business and government leaders, and pastors and church leaders. The university students had been very receptive, but I sensed the professors were quite skeptical. I stood and began to declare the love of Christ to the professors. Following my presentation, they asked many questions, most tinged with skepticism. The first professor to vocalize his skepticism asked about the atrocities committed in the name of Christ throughout history. All subsequent questions were of the same nature.

Later another professor spoke up, revealing the root of their skepticism. "You know, Mr. Tippit, many of us have lost faith in the church. When the atrocities were committed here in Rwanda, some of the church leaders told the people that they would be safe in the church. When Tutsis came to the church for a place of refuge, the priest or pastor called for the militia to come. The militias came and slaughtered the people. How can we ever trust the church again?"

RELIGION VERSUS A RELATIONSHIP

I reasoned with them that there was a great difference between religion and a relationship with God. "Many of those who participated in the atrocities were churchmen. But there's a big difference in being a churchman and being a Christian." I continued to try to explain the difference between genuine Christianity and surface religion. "Religion kills and destroys," I said. "But Jesus brings life and peace to the human heart."

I could tell that they were having a hard time swallowing my reasoning. When tragedy strikes the heart, reason many times goes out the window, and beliefs are often built on the shifting foundation of emotional hurt.

When the professors had finished their questioning, the chancellor, Deogratius Kayumba, stood and very respectfully said, "Mr. Tippit, you have done a good job of answering our questions tonight. But there's one question for which I still don't have a satisfactory answer. Where was the church? Where was the church during the atrocities?"

Of course, that question was rhetorical. We all knew where a segment of the church was during the genocide. They participated in it. But then Kayumba asked an even more penetrating question. "Where was the church *before* the genocide?" he asked. "Why wasn't the church building a foundation of love in the hearts of people that would have protected society from such atrocities?"

His question cut deeply into my heart. A couple of days later the question gripped me even more, as I visited a church site where five thousand people were senselessly slaughtered. There I felt a little of the pain of the Rwandan people.

"Where was the church?" Why did the church participate in such great atrocities? The question, asked by the chancellor echoed in my mind, and it echoes through the years. Where is the church during great acts of atrocity? The answer, sadly, is that sometimes it has participated in them. At other times the church has quietly condoned or ignored them, including the classic instance of World War II in Nazi Germany. There only a few Christians and churches willingly opposed nazism; most feared the persecution and responded to the intimidation and threats of imprisonment.

Indeed, more harm has been done to the name of Christ by religious people who have no genuine relationship with God—or a shallow, superficial one—than by all the questions that skeptics outside the church have ever asked. Most legitimate questions of the skeptics don't deal with the nature of Christ. Most of them deal with the un-Christlike behavior of those who claim to be His followers.

The church must have a deep commitment not to compromise the Christian life and ethic. The transformed Christian, empowered by the Holy Spirit to demonstrate sincere love to other believers—and to his enemies—will draw people who want to escape the coming storm. Followers of Christ who show such love will contrast strongly with the division and bitterness among national, racial, and ethnic groups described in chapters 1 and 3. Such love is possible; it reflects our growing in the character of Christ, becoming more like Him.

THE POWER TO LOVE
THOSE WHO OPPOSE US

Christ gives us the power to love even those who reject and despise us. It's easy to love those who love us. The non-

Christian world can do that. But it takes the power and love of Christ to love those who oppose us. Yet that is the way we disarm the skeptics and let them see the message of God's love through us.

In Struga, Macedonia, a woman called me during a live radio program to describe her spiritual condition. "I believe in God," she said. "But I have begun to doubt the existence of God. The people closest to me have rejected me because of my faith in God. What can I do? I'm almost ready to give up my faith."

If we allow Christ to control us, then His grace is applied to our hearts. We then experience the transforming power of Christ.

"The real evidence of the existence of God lies in this one great truth," I replied. "Christ gives us the power to love those who hate us; to accept those that reject us; and to be kind to those who try to harm us. If we allow Christ to control us, then His grace is applied to our hearts. We then experience the transforming power of Christ. It's in that transformation of our inner man that we see the proof of God's existence. The evidence is within your mind and soul. It's Christ in you. His presence in your innermost being changing you is the great confirmation of His reality."

That truth encouraged the Macedonian woman, but it is not just for her; "Christ in you" has enabled the church to walk through the most difficult moments of history. From the early followers of Christ until this day, the indwelling presence of Christ has been the fountain of life that has filled Christians during dry and thirsty moments. Early Christians were fed to the lions. Yet, they were able to love their persecutors. Others were burned at the stake. But the more the world was filled with hate and anger, the more Christians were filled with love and peace. Their testimonies were filled with the sweet fragrance of the transforming power of Christ. Consequently, the gospel spread throughout the Roman empire.

WHEN PERSONAL FAITH
BECOMES INSTITUTIONAL FAITH

Interestingly, an institutional version of Christianity that changed the focus from a relationship with Christ to an understanding of rules and emphasis on the institution, came two centuries later, when Constantine supposedly was converted to Christ though a vision he had of a cross. In A.D. 312 he was engaged in a battle with his rival Maxentius. Although Constantine had been a worshiper of the "Unconquered Sun," he attributed his victory in the battle to the God of the Christians. According to church father Eusebius and based on Constantine's own later testimony, the emperor saw a vision of the cross in the sky the night before a key battle in which he was commanded to mark his soldiers' shields with the monogram of Christ. Therefore the emperor had the monogram, consisting of the two initial letters of the Greek name of Christ—X (ch) and P (r) —placed atop an image of a cross and set upon his standard.[1]

Constantine's method was a big departure from the teachings of Christ. The church ceased to change the world by the power of God's love. It now began to march with the power of the sword. The church began looking to a man for its strength and victory rather than God, and the Christian faith became known as a religious institution as much as a personal faith in Jesus Christ. In 325 Constantine presided at the Council of Nicaea, even though he was unbaptized at the time. The church entered a new period of history. It became friends with the culture and began to adapt the ways and methods of culture rather than the character of Christ. Instead of the church changing the world, the world transformed the church. The reason that the world conquered the church was simply because the church ceased to be conquered by Christ.

Ritual and religion replaced a vital relationship with Christ. Consequently the world entered the "dark age," and the light of the church ceased to burn brightly.

The church began to operate by outward form rather than inward transformation. The church became conformed to the world. It grew large. It grew quickly. It grew into the image of the world rather than the image of Christ. Ritual and religion replaced a vital relationship with Christ. Consequently the world entered the "dark age," and the light of the church ceased to burn brightly. Although a remnant remained of those who would hold Christ and His words as their standard, it wasn't until the Reformation, hundreds of years later, that the church would begin to recapture the power that had made it a bright shining light in a dark world.

Reformers throughout Europe began to preach the truth of the Bible. Men such as John Calvin of Switzerland, John Knox of Scotland, and Martin Luther of Germany were enlightened by the truth of the Scriptures. They began calling the church to return to the Bible. Hearts again began to be transformed by God's power. Lives were changed and the church once again began to change the world rather than be changed by the world. The light of the gospel once again began to burn brightly. The church again became distinctive in society. It still had a long way to go, but the Reformation was a beginning.

As we draw near to the close of church history, the church must once again recapture its distinctive. We must be world-changers rather than being changed by the corrupted system of the world. We must be conquered by Christ in our inner man before we will be able to capture the hearts of men and women in need of Christ. It's easy and very tempting to conform to the standards of this world system. But in the long run, that will produce much great damage to the testimony of the Christian church.

THE CHRISTIAN RESPONSE TO RACISM AND ETHNIC HATRED

As we approach the close of the twentieth century and the imminent return of Christ, we will see a continual rise of "nation against nation" as nationalism continues to increase. Ethnic and racial conflict will abound. This will give Christians an opportunity to manifest the transforming power of Christ. We have the ability to cross those boundaries of racism and ethnic hatred because of the power of the indwelling Christ. It's then imperative that genuine Christians be transformed in their innermost beings to the image of Christ rather than conformed to the culture around us (Romans 12:2; 2 Corinthians 4:16). That may produce temporary animosity from the culture surrounding us. But ultimately we will be "called the sons of God" (Matthew 5:9).

Sadly, some Christians are more committed to cultural prejudices than biblical mandates. Those preferences become prejudices, independent of and often hostile to the Scriptures.

I grew up in the deep southern part of the United States at a time of great racial tensions. During my junior year of high school, our school was integrated for the first time, as four African-American students courageously entered our school. One day a group of white students encircled a black girl during the lunch hour and began to shout. The girl just began to weep. Even though I wasn't a Christian, I knew that terrible injustice was being committed by my classmates.

When I opened my life by faith to Christ during my freshman year of college, I knew I would never be the same. One of the first changes that He made in my heart was in my attitudes towards those of different racial backgrounds. For the first time in my life, I didn't see people as black or white; I only saw them as unique individuals created in the image of God and I began to understand the dignity of all people. But I also learned not all Christians accepted that fact.

Many racial attitudes held by white Christians are unbiblical and not Christlike. . . . There must be deep repentance in the hearts of God's people for revival to occur.

Many of the white churches in southern Louisiana wouldn't permit blacks into their worship services. If any black Christians attempted to come and worship, they were viewed as troublemakers. During those days, the various institutions were separated racially. I began to go to an

African-American orphanage and play basketball with some of the young people. We had Bible studies together. It was a great time early in my Christian life. But some people close to me thought that I had been brainwashed by Martin Luther King. They were wrong. Instead, I had been heart-washed by the King of Kings.

I quickly came to understand that many Christians had been more influenced by culture than by Christ. I'm convinced that before a great spiritual revival can come to parts of the southern United States, the sin of racism must be confessed and dealt with thoroughly. Such racism is not confined to the Deep South, though. Subtle racism permeates churches in much of the United States. That may be why the growing Promise Keepers movement is succeeding: one of its goals is to end racial divisions among Christians, establishing relationships among black, Hispanic, Asian, and white men. It calls for repentance among white Christians to their minority brothers. Many racial attitudes held by white Christians are unbiblical and not Christlike, and there must be deep repentance in the hearts of God's people for revival to occur.

As the racial and ethnic gaps grow in the hearts of men and women in these last days, we must ask the same question that the chancellor of the National University of Rwanda asked: "Where is the church?" In a day in which Africans, Europeans, Americans, and Asians are being pitted against one another, Christians must be the salt of the earth and the light of the world. We must cross the boundaries of ethnic and racial conflict so that the world will know that we are Christ's followers by the love that we have for one another.

There must be a new sense of transparency and honesty among God's people. We must allow the Holy Spirit to search our hearts and show us where we have become like our culture rather than like Christ. We must never yield to the shifting whims of cultural leaders who would pit race against race and ethnic group against ethnic group. This is no time to follow extremists on the right or the left, no matter how charismatic those leaders may be. We should follow only a leader who observes biblical guidelines, who himself has only one captain: the Lord of Lords.

True spirituality will never oppose Christian morality. The two must harmonize with each other in order to give rise to Christlike behavior. It's the "renewing of the mind" (Romans 12:2) that produces conformity into the image of Christ in our inner person. This inward renewal then becomes a safeguard against a system of thought in the world that is contrary to the nature and character of God. As we allow Christ to alter our thought processes, we will then begin to live in the manner in which we were created to live. He is the center point that protects us from extremes and aberrations of true Christianity.

STANDING AGAINST
A WAYWARD CULTURE

But there will always be a cultural system surrounding us that will attempt to mold us and modify our behavior into that which will ultimately destroy us. The closer the gathering storm comes, the darker and more deadly we can expect the hour to become. When God created man, the first institution that He established was that of marriage. All societal relationships would grow out of that institution. The well-being of society would be directly related to the health of the family. However, when Adam and Eve disobeyed God and stepped outside His authority, they opened themselves up to a storm that would devastate their family as well as families for generations to come. One of their children (Cain) senselessly killed his brother (Abel). If mankind was divided and at war in that most basic unit of society, then certainly society would reap the deadly harvest of hatred. That crop of animosity has been passed through the generations until we have a civilization on the verge of a storm previously unknown in human history.

Perhaps the ultimate test of conformity into the image of Christ lies in how we treat those closest to us, our family members. The opposite is also true. Adam and Eve's insubordination to the authority of God produced catastrophe among those whom they loved and cared about. From the beginning, sin caused brother to turn against brother. The Bible indicates that same spirit of lawlessness will grow until it becomes the spirit of the age prior to Christ's return.

In a practical sense that means the most basic institution of society, the family, will experience great upheaval and tragedy. Already, modern society is flaunting its rebellion against God and shaking its fist in God's face by denying His character and destroying the first institution that He created. The characteristic of this age is the worldwide breakdown of the family unit. Much of the darkness in modern civilization can be attributed to its collapse.

As traditional biblical values have been rejected by Western societies in the past thirty years, the family has become one of the biggest casualties. Live-in sexual relationships, once frowned upon, have became a normal part of Western culture. That has brought unwanted pregnancies and some tough choices. One solution has been abortion, and with its legalization in many countries, including the United States in 1973, parents have been able to kill their future offspring. Millions of unwanted babies have been voluntarily aborted around the world. Freedom of choice overtook freedom of the child in the womb to live.

With biblical sexual morality no longer the norm of the day, certain behavior went from being wrong to being labeled an "alternative lifestyle." In America, homosexuals came out of the closet and gained political clout and strength. Homosexual and lesbian churches were formed. Freedom of choice became the moral standard and relativity the philosophy of the day. In the hearts of many, "choice" concerning the birth of children became more precious than "life" and certainly more precious than the absolute nature of God.

"WHERE IS THE CHURCH?"

The question of the chancellor of the university in Rwanda can be asked today: "Where is the church?" In the midst of growing darkness throughout the world, the church should be laying down the moral and biblical foundation in society. Unfortunately, much of the church seems to be absorbed with the darkness rather than dispelling it. Just as some of the Rwandan church people placed their ethnicity above their Christianity, many in the Western church have compromised themselves with the moral standards of a culture that opposes the character of God.

In Little Rock, Arkansas, in early 1995 hundreds of pastors and leaders from throughout the United States attended a national congress on revival and spiritual awakening within the American Christian community. One pastor, who I'll call Reverend Conway, told participants at the congress about a dilemma his church recognized as they considered how to bring a spiritual awakening to their community and the nation. What occurred exemplifies the state of the church today.

Reverend Conway's church was planning to have a series of meetings with "Life Action Ministries," an organization dedicated to calling churches in North America to revival. In preparation for the meetings, the church conducted a series of prayer meetings. They decided to pray about the sins that were so prevalent in American culture and to pray for God to bring moral renewal to the land. They listed many of the moral evils in the land, including crime, racism, abortion, homosexuality, adultery, and drug abuse. They then prayed that God would change the moral climate of the nation.

After they prayed about the sins of the nation, they began to make a list of the sins that were present within their own church. They discovered that every sin they had listed in the nation was in their church. Then Reverend Conway began to weep as he confessed to the Little Rock conference that *he* had been involved in an affair with another woman. He concluded by stating that he and his church had conformed to the world system. He told of their repentance and God's forgiveness.

I wish that his testimony was unusual. However, I'm convinced that the state of his congregation has become more of a norm today. In many instances there's as much darkness in the church as outside it.

As we look upon the horizon of the close of human history, we can see a gathering storm. It's absolutely imperative that Christians determine to follow Christ rather than culture. The beacon that will shine brightly and attract the spiritually searching millions will be the transformed Christian. You can be that beacon, and so can I. Those who have fallen greatly, such as Pastor Conway, can be that beacon as well. That's part of the joy of God's grace—it restores and lifts us up, and people are attracted by the change they see. But such a beacon must stand on a solid foundation. The standard must be the solid foundation of the Bible and not the shifting sands of the latest cultural philosophy.

The time has come for Christians to determine to follow the teachings of Christ instead of the fashionable ways of pluralism and secularism. The times demand it. Christ commands it. Christians must settle it—once and for all. Such transformed Christians will stand out and give hope as the gathering storm approaches.

Christians are not distinguished from the rest of mankind either in locality or in speech or in customs. . . . They live in their own home-towns, but only as sojourners; they bear their share of all things as citizens, but endure hardships as foreigners. Every foreign land is home to them, and every home is foreign. . . . They love all, and are persecuted by all.[1]

Anonymous
Epistle to Diognetus,
mid–second century

Then Jesus came to them and said, "All authority in heaven and on earth has been given to me. Therefore go and make disciples of all nations, baptizing them in the name of the Father and of the Son and of the Holy Spirit, and teaching them to obey everything I have commanded you. And surely I am with you always, to the very end of the age."

Matthew 28:18–20

Chapter Eleven

....

COMPASSIONATE EVANGELISM

A few years ago I stood before hundreds of high-caste Hindus in a district where there was not one Christian in a region populated with millions. I spoke to the workers about the creation and rebellion of man. I told them of the Savior who was sent from the one true and living God to forgive their sins and wrongs. As I spoke of how Jesus took the punishment for our sins when He died on the cross, these high-caste Hindus broke into applause. A few days later I brought a similar message to the streets of another wholly Hindu city. A man stepped out of the crowd which was gathered around me and extended a hand to shake. "I want to thank you for coming such a long way," he said, "to bring us this good news."

The gospel of Christ truly is good news. There's very little good news in the world today, but the message of God's love for a sinful world stands as a bright and shining light on a planet covered by spiritual and moral darkness. It's that message that has compelled me to go to the peoples and nations of the world. It's that great story that has constrained me to spend my life crossing political, cultural, racial, and geographic boundaries. I've come to understand a little of what the apostle Paul meant when he said, "I am obligated both to Greeks and non-Greeks, both to the wise and the foolish. . . . I am not ashamed of the gospel, because it is the power of God for the salvation of everyone who believes: first for the Jew, then for the Gentile" (Romans 1:14, 16).

The love of God is so great that it knows no boundaries. It's so broad that it speaks every language. It's so strong that it shatters the strong prejudices of nationalism and racism. It's so penetrating that it's able to heal the deepest wounds of the broken heart. That love flows from the throne of God to the hurts of humanity. It's the spring of life that enters all who believe and receive Christ into their lives. Such great love can rebuild demolished lives and shape them into magnificent trophies of God's grace.

But the tragedy of this great love is that most of the world is void of any knowledge of it. Sometimes my heart breaks when I see so many comfortable Christians who have been greatly blessed by God, but have no interest in sharing His love with the hurting world around them. I find myself overwhelmed with the burden of the lostness of the world. There is an urgency to proclaiming the good news of God's love in Christ. As the storm clouds cross the horizon of human history, the Christian community must be mobilized and motivated to reach the world. Someone has said that Christian evangelism is simply "one beggar telling another beggar where to find bread." I believe that the times in which we live demand an even stronger definition than that. It's one dying person telling another dying person where to find the One who is the resurrection and the life.

THE DISTINCT MESSAGE OF THE FINAL DAYS

The closer we come to that great climactic moment in history when Christ shall return, the more we can expect to see devastation in the lives of people. That will present an unprecedented opportunity to share the good news with a needy world. All of the world and local news will be so terrible that the good news of Christ's love will become like a stream of living water in the midst of a desert. There are two distinct characteristics of those who will be used of God to minister to those in need during the last days. First, they will be a people with uncompromised convictions concerning moral values. Second, they will be a compassionate people. They will be able to reach out in love to those who stand against everything for which they stand.

Announced with Conviction

Uncompromising convictions and compassion will go hand in hand, for an unyielding message must be tempered with love. Consider a current program underway in Hungary. Campus Crusade for Christ developed a high school educational program called Youth at the Threshold of Life (YTL) to help teens understand self-image, sex in the age of AIDS, relationship, and character development. A Hungarian Campus Crusade staff member wrote to a friend of a friend, explaining his work with students and how the YTL curriculum might help Hungary in the fight against AIDS. The "friend of a friend" was Denes Banhegyi, AIDS coordinator at Hungary's National Institute of Health. Banhegyi was impressed with what he heard, even though he was not a Christian. Consequently, Hungary's Campus Crusade was allowed to develop a national program promoting Christian moral values and present the gospel of Christ.

Dr. Banhegyi remarked, "We have different opinions on some things, but we can work together because we agree where it really counts—helping the younger generation. This is not only an AIDS prevention program, nor a sexual health program. It shows young people how to live, how to find their place in society."[2]

Campus Crusade has reported many coming to Christ through the program begun in Hungary. David Robinson, a crusade staff member, said, "Those who hear the gospel through this program are saying, 'I can't believe there is water in this desert.' "[3]

Announced with Compassion

As the gathering storm approaches and people feel increasingly needy, Christians must also announce the gospel with compassion. A desperately hurting world will welcome Christ's love when it is presented with compassion. For instance, after a college friend died of AIDS in 1991, Deb Jones responded with compassion by becoming a counselor at Camp Heartland, a summer camp for children with HIV. Deb had a full-time position with a national Christian organization, but after her friend's death she devoted much of her time to assisting at fund-raisers, speaking at AIDS conferences, and serving at a center for HIV/AIDS patients.

The greatest thing a person can do with his life is to find out what God is up to in his generation and commit his life to that. [Those who do will find themselves] on the cutting edge of what God is doing in this generation.

"For many who are involved in immoral sexual behavior, the consequence often manifested is HIV and AIDS," she told an interviewer. "Yet every person who does not enter into a relationship with Christ is going to spend eternity away from God, whether they die today or thirty years from now. If Christ were here today, I think He would be in the middle of these situations. He wouldn't bend on the sin issue, but He wouldn't back away from the love issue."[4]

Those who stand, like Deb, on a strong biblical foundation of morality and reach out in God's love to a hurting world around them will impact society greatly in these last days. It's not just large Christian agencies that can be a bright and shining light in the darkness that's engulfing civilization. Every Christian can play a vital role in the fulfillment of the Great Commission of Christ. I've met common, ordinary individuals who understood the uniqueness of the times in which we are living. They've committed themselves to bringing the gospel to a lost and dying world, and God is greatly using them. Many local churches are catching a vision of their part in the fulfillment of Christ's commission during these last days.

Someone once said to me that the greatest thing a person can do with his life is to find out what God is up to in his generation and commit his life to that. As we see the storm clouds on the horizon of history, there's one thing that's absolutely certain. There will be one last great thrust of the gospel around the world before Christ returns. The people, churches, and organizations that give themselves to that cause will be on the cutting edge of what God is doing in this generation. The following are a few examples of those that have understood this truth and are practicing it.

THE CHURCH IN ACTION

Churches have many resources for displaying compassion. Although churches may seem to be only institutions, we must remember churches are people—the people of God—and those people using appropriate resources can enact a compassionate and powerful type of evangelism. Here are three.

In a University Town

In 1987 the Highland Baptist Church in Waco, Texas, began to recognize the tremendous opportunities in world evangelization. Church members knew that they were sitting on a spiritual gold mine in resources: thousands of young adults attended nearby Baylor University. Many of them were searching for God's plan for their lives, but really didn't know where to begin their journey.

The assistant singles pastor began to challenge many of the students to follow Christ completely, trying to develop in them a world vision. The church began a nine-month missions/discipleship internship with some of the students. During the first six months students focused on personal growth and local outreach. Then the assistant singles pastor and other church members led the interns oversees to a pioneer mission area. Since then, Highland Baptist has started churches in Mongolia and Siberia. They now have full-time missionaries in those areas who were trained and equipped through their intern program.

Some of the young people have felt a call into full-time Christian ministry. Others have entered the secular workplace, but have done so with a keen understanding of what God wants to do with them during these historic times. After my son, Dave, had completed most of his courses for a degree in finance from Baylor University, a friend challenged him to take a missions internship at the church. Dave agreed and served in Mongolia and Siberia through the internship program. He came back a changed person. Even though he grew up in a Christian home that was committed to world evangelization, it wasn't until he personally went on a mission to the unreached regions of the world that he embraced the vision of world evangelism. He surrendered his life to the call of international evangelism. It has been a thrill for me to watch him catch a vision to reach the world.

I heard the youth pastor of this church define the purpose of the program: "Our vision is to see young people come to love Jesus Christ so much that they could never turn away from Him, and to see those young people have God's vision for the world."

In the City

In San Antonio, Alamo City Christian Fellowship decided to show God's love in the community by beginning a ministry called Support Saturday. Members of the congregation were asked to bring not only their financial tithes and offerings but also clothes and food each Sunday. The church initiated a feeding and clothing center for the needy of the community. During 1995 the church distributed nearly one million pounds of food to hungry people. Many church members gave up their Saturdays to assist the poor and needy at the center. Some auto mechanics offered free work on the cars of widows and single mothers during the Saturday operating hours.

As a result the church has been able to reach many in San Antonio with the gospel. It's become one of the fastest-growing churches in the United States. Regular attendance has grown from six hundred in 1987 to more than three thousand in 1995. In the United States, other city churches as well are discovering that such community projects exemplify Christ's love. These projects give many opportunities to invite recipients to their churches and to present the gospel in non-church settings.

In an International Community

The Church on Brady in East Los Angeles continues to change and adapt to fit the needs of a changing city. In their compassion, church leaders have never compromised their convictions or changed the message of the need for salvation through Jesus Christ. Instead members have shown sensitivity as the surrounding population has become an international community. This has meant sacrifice and adoption, but a loving people have done that.

In 1969 the largely Anglo congregation did not reflect its dominant Mexican-American community in East Los Angeles. Church attendance was only seventy-five when new pastor Tom Wolf arrived.

Pastor Wolf believed that in an unlikely place like East L.A. the church could have a global impact. He began developing strategies to reach the Hispanic population. The church grew throughout the 1970s and peaked in the early 1980s with five hundred attending weekly. Compassion and love were the hallmarks of the church, and the community had responded. But soon the community was changing again. Many Asians had moved in to join the dominant Hispanic and minority Anglo populations. To meet the needs of the changing world of East L.A., the church shifted from a Sunday school-based education program to a small-cell concept that appealed to many Asian residents.

In 1992 new pastor Erwin McManus continued the pastoral vision for reaching the world locally, through a church surrounded by many immigrants. Like many urban centers, East L.A. now includes Hispanics, Asians, Indians, and Pakistanis. "I am ministering to people who are worshiping false gods," Pastor McManus said. "Many are Hindus, Muslims, and Buddhists. But the church has made an intentional decision to reach out to these people and show them the love of Christ."

McManus, himself a native of El Salvador, leads a congregation who recognizes the opportunity to reach the world by reaching the surrounding community. The Church on Brady's mission statement targets the church as "a spiritual reference point east of downtown L.A. and a sending base to the ends of the earth." With church attendance at more than seven hundred, many from the congregation have left as missionaries to other countries; Pastor McManus sees church members as meeting basic people needs.

"When you deal in a world in which people don't know Christ, you must understand that there are three basic human needs—to believe, to become, and to belong. The body of Christ has the answer to these needs—faith, hope, and love. We must reach out to a non-Christian community with those three solutions."[5]

INDIVIDUALS IN ACTION

Compassion begins with individuals, of course. Here are ways individuals show a heart for evangelism by using specific gifts.

Through Short-Term Missions Service

Marshall, a friend in Oregon, asked if he could travel with me on a ministry trip to Africa. "That would great," I said. During his visit, Marshall described his vision to reach the world.

"Every year I take vacation time and go on a mission trip to a different part of the world," he said. I was impressed but wondered how difficult it was for him to get the time off from work to do that. His answer reminded me how compassion often requires sacrifice.

"For several years, it wasn't any problem," he said. "Then I was offered a promotion. It meant that I could make much more money. I accepted the position. But, I quickly learned that the company couldn't afford to have me away from the office for two weeks at a time. So, I went back to my employer and told him that I would prefer to be demoted back to my original position.

"My boss had a real hard time understanding that. But he did it, and I'm able to continue to take my two weeks each year and travel to different areas of the world and share my testimony of what Christ has done for me."

Marshall had radically right priorities. God's mission took precedent over material possessions.

Through Skills

"Sammy, I'm not an evangelist like you. But God has given me gifts and abilities that I believe He wants to use for His glory in reaching our world for Christ." The businessman sat across from me in a restaurant as he shared his vision for using his business skills for Christ. He had bought an elephant for a Bible school in Burma, he said. Then he helped the school to understand some basic principles of business.

With his gifts of the elephant and training, the school has since developed a lumber mill and uses the elephant to haul lumber out of the forests. Consequently, the Bible college students have become self-supporting. This Christian businessman is now helping Christian leaders in various developing nations of the world to learn how to become self-supporting.

Through Prayer

When my wife and I are at home, she attends a women's prayer group every Tuesday afternoon. These women are, in my opinion, some of the real heroes of the faith. They have a lot of domestic responsibilities with their families, but they haven't forgotten the needs of the world. They have set a very clear agenda for their prayer group. They pray specifically for two things. They pray for spiritual awakening in our community and nation. Secondly, they pray for world evangelization. I don't know of any group of people who have had such a profound impact on my ministry of reaching the world for Christ.

The ministry of prayer is a powerful way for individuals to show compassion to missionaries and the masses, for prayer beseeches the mighty hand of God to help. In my wife's group, the ministry of prayer has become so effective that when missionaries come to our city, many of them want to meet with this group and seek their prayer support.

Through Financial Gifts

A Christian friend said to me, "Sammy, God has given me a gift and ability to make money. I want to use that gift for His glory and His kingdom. Because of my responsibilities, I can't go to places like you go. But I can help you to go to those places." That Christian businessman has been a major supporter of our ministry since that time. He and others like him have helped us to reach multitudes of people in nations around the world.

I believe that when we get to heaven, there will be thousands of people from distant regions of the globe who will be there because of the generosity of men and women like this businessman. Christians in the Western world need to desperately rethink their financial priorities in light of the unique opportunities in this generation for world evangelization.

THE CHURCH IN
THE EASTERN HEMISPHERE

Lest you think that missions is a Western enterprise, let me assure you that compassionate evangelism includes African, Asian, and Eastern European Christians. When one dying person wants to help another dying person find life, nationality does not matter. Here's one example from

Romania. The Immanuel Bible Institute in Oradea, Romania, has emerged in the 1990s as a model of what Eastern Europeans can do for the cause of world evangelization if provided with the necessary resources. Once dominated by the communist government's official atheism, believers here and in other churches and schools are zealous now to proclaim the good news in other countries as well as their own. In 1991 God opened the door for me ito travel to unreached regions of Siberia. A handful of Christians in Norilsk, a Russian city located above the Arctic circle, asked if we would conduct a citywide evangelistic meeting in the local soccer stadium

Such a task of evangelism would have been impossible without the vision of the Immanuel Bible Institute in Oradea. School administrators allowed twenty students, all from former Soviet republics, to take a month to travel to Siberia with me. They did all of the preparation work for the evangelistic meetings. Then, they stayed after I left the city to work with the new believers. Because of the large response to the gospel, two of the students were permitted to stay for more than a year to disciple and help establish a church for the new believers. Our ministry provided the financial support for the students, and the Bible institute provided a system of accountability for them. Subsequently, some of the new Siberian Christians have gone to study at Immanuel Bible Institute and plan to return to their region of Siberia to continue bringing the message of the gospel.

YOUR INVOLVEMENT

The preceding examples show that every Christian can be a part of fulfilling the Great Commission. As history rapidly heads towards the culmination of time, it will become more evident that Christians have the only news that is truly good news. The light of the gospel will shine more brightly with every passing day, even as the days grow darker morally. God's light will always shine brightly on the eve of the storm.

I would rather be alive today than any other time in human history. Modern communication and transportation offer us great opportunity to complete the task given by Christ to His church. Yet every Christian is needed in the task of world evangelization.

It's not enough to say, "I'll give a little money and that's sufficient." Every Christian must take a long hard look at his life and discover what gifts and resources God has placed within him. It may be that the primary contribution of some will be financial. But we must be careful not to delegate the responsibility of world evangelization to a few superstars. Every Christian needs to be a student of missions. Every true follower of Christ needs to take upon himself the burden of prayer for the unreached peoples of the world. And every believer must look around him and see what Jesus saw when the Scriptures said, "When he saw the crowds, he had compassion on them, because they were harassed and helpless, like sheep without a shepherd" (Matthew 9:36).

Today is the day for compassionate evangelism. The harvest is ripe. Look around you. Hurting people are everywhere. You don't have to go all the way to Mongolia to find them. John Wesley used to say, "The world is my parish." That could never more be true than today. The Church on Brady in East Los Angeles has discovered that the world is on the move. We no longer have to go to the world. God has brought the world to us. The face of North America and Western Europe has dramatically changed. I spoke recently at a university in Toronto, Canada. There 90 percent of the students to whom I spoke were of Asian origin.

It's a new day. Sin is taking its toll and wrecking lives. Families are being destroyed. The deadly disease, AIDS, is multiplying. Crime is rising. False messiahs are emerging.

War is spreading. Natural disasters appear to be increasing in frequency. In the midst of this kind of world, the gospel truly is good news. And every Christian has been entrusted with that good news and given the responsibility to share it.

Christians affirm the infallibility and inerrancy of the Bible because God is ultimately the author of the Bible. And because God is incapable of inspiring falsehood, His word is altogether true and trustworthy. Any normally prepared human literary product is liable to error. But the Bible is not a normal human project. If the Bible is inspired and superintended by God, then it cannot err.[1]

R. C. Sproul

"Whoever has my commands and obeys them, he is the one who loves me. He who loves me will be loved by my Father, and I too will love him and show myself to him."

John 14:21

Chapter Twelve

....

STANDING
IN THE STORM

The Russians pulled out of Cuba when the Soviet Union collapsed, but they left one thing behind—a small car called the Lada. Hundreds of these vehicles roamed the Cuban countryside, and recently five North Americans, including myself, were stuffed in one of the small Russian automobiles with our luggage to drive the bumpy roads of eastern Cuba. As rough as our Lada ride was, I found the conversation with the local driver uplifting.

"I didn't know that Christianity existed in Cuba until six years ago," our driver began. "I thought that Castro had wiped the church off the face of Cuba during the 1960s. But six years ago I met some Christians, and they invited me to go to church with them. I was amazed to find the church filled with people. Not long afterwards I came to know Christ in a personal way."

His story wasn't much different from many stories that I heard. The first time I went to Cuba in March 1994, I sensed an enthusiasm about Christ. Churches were filled and overflowing. When I returned six months later, some of the same churches had experienced tremendous growth. At one church, the pews were packed. I thought the church had placed a huge rectangular mirror behind the pulpit, for part of the front wall seemed to be missing. I soon realized that the "mirror" was a large opening in the center of the front wall, with hundreds of faces staring back to the platform. The church leaders had cut a rectangular hole in the wall behind the pulpit; behind the wall was another room filled with people seated exactly as they were in the auditorium. I had to preach both directions that night! That church had almost doubled within six months.

CUBA AND ROMANIA:
THE POWER OF PERSECUTION

Cuba is one of two places in the world where I experienced a powerful style of evangelism and church growth. I first observed such evangelism in Romania just before the fall of the evil dictator, Ceaucescu. The churches were so packed during our meetings that pastors asked the people not to come into the auditoriums. They asked Christians to stand outside and allow the non-Christians seating space in the auditorium. I would then preach in sanctuaries packed with nonbelievers, hungry for the message of hope. Many came to Christ. One night, for instance, the Romanian pastor arrived late for the services. The church was so crammed with people that the pastor couldn't even get into the auditorium for the sevices!

What is the common denominator that made evangelism so powerful? The key common trait in Cuba, Romania, and much of Eastern Europe is the persecution that Christians had to overcome. In these countries, Christians have endured extremely harsh times because of their faith. These believers did not merely survive severe persecution, they triumphed. During the darkest moments of their history, they endured and grew. You really learn the character of people when they go through trials.

During December 1995, church leaders invited me to preach in churches throughout the eastern half of Cuba. A day after speaking in Holguin, Cuba's fourth-largest city, I received a message at my hotel: report to the office of Immigration and Foreign Affairs at 11:30 that morning.

When Cliff Liese, my interpreter, and I arrived at the office, we were told that I had broken the law by speaking publicly in the churches. "Do not speak again or you will face serious consequences," the officials threatened. They drafted a report of my "activities" and sent it to Havana. I had to sign the report stating that I clearly understood the warning that had been given to me.

The young pastor looked me straight in the eyes and said, "Sammy, this is what we go through all the time. I've been called in several times by the authorities. But I refuse to give in to them."

Cliff and I went immediately from the government offices to the home of the pastor. His church had experienced rapid growth. I told the pastor that I didn't want to do anything to hurt him or his church. The young pastor looked me straight in the eyes and said, "Sammy, this is what we go through all the time. I've been called in several times by the authorities. But I refuse to give in to them. Our church is growing, and I will continue to preach and minister the Word of God as long as God gives me the strength to do it. We need you to stand with us in these days. It's very important to us." The pastor then went to the authorities and lodged a formal protest about what they had done to me.

"You have violated our human rights, and you've interfered in the internal affairs of our church," he told the government officials. "We ask that you drop the threats that you have made against our guest and allow him to speak."

However, the authorities weren't so accommodating. They told the pastor, "Mr. Tippit can only bring a greeting, but he cannot enter the pulpit and preach."

When we arrived at the church immediately before the services were to begin, the pastor told me what transpired in his conversation with the officials. "I will tell the people what has happened to you," he added, "and then ask you to bring a greeting from the bench where you are seated. You can then do whatever you feel God wants you to do. Just know that I am willing to suffer any consequences. Don't be concerned about me."

When the pastor told the congregation what happened to Cliff and myself, a gasp went through the auditorium. He then asked me to greet the people. For the next twenty-five minutes, I brought greetings and shared testimony and Scripture from my church bench. You could see the smiles on the faces of the Christians. Many of them came to me after the service smiling and saying, "Good 'greeting sermon,' Pastor Sammy."

The next morning we decided that it would be prudent to leave the city. However, a pastor from a rural area showed up at our hotel. People had walked for miles to his church to hear me preach. He pleaded with me to come. I told him that it would be very dangerous for me to preach there.

"I'm willing to suffer anything," the pastor replied. "But there are many people waiting to hear the gospel. You must come and preach the good news to them."

I had no other choice. I had to go with him. The little country church was packed. People were standing outside and completely encircled the church. I preached the good news. Many decided to follow Christ at the close of my message. We left there and returned to Santiago. I was scheduled to preach the next two evenings in Bayamo, a city about two hours away. We decided that it would not be safe to stay in Bayamo. I would go there and preach but return to Santiago immediately after the service.

When I arrived in Bayamo, I told the pastor what had transpired in Holguin. I showed him the document prohibiting my preaching. I then said, "Pastor, I have come to Cuba for only one purpose. I've come to glorify God and be a servant to the Cuban people. I don't want to do anything to hurt you or your ministry. We don't have to go through with this meeting tonight. If you feel we need to cancel it, then I understand. But I'm available to you. I'll do whatever you think is best."

The pastor smiled at me and gently said, "Sammy, I've been arrested more than one time. I'm not afraid. It will do more harm to us if you don't preach tonight than if you do preach. The communists want to see if you will stand with us in our sufferings, or if you will run the first time there's a threat."

His words sealed my decision. I had to preach. I really had no other choice. These men walked in a depth of obedience that few Christians in my own country know. Their commitment to Christ reminded me of the commitment of so many in Eastern Europe who stood firmly for Christ during the dark days of communism. I've learned so much from those believers. They not only survived a systematic attempt to exterminate Christianity from their lands, but they have also emerged as "more than conquerors through Christ." Instead of a church that shut its doors and gave up in the midst of adversity, believers remained faithful and grew during affliction.

Lessons to Learn

I believe that we can learn from Christians in Cuba, Eastern Europe, and other difficult areas of the world. As I noted in chapter 8, persecution has come, and it will continue. We can expect it. Evil seems to be making unprecedented strides at the close of the twentieth century. How then shall we live in such dark times? I believe that we can look to the suffering church for the answer to that question. They have learned to live by eternal principles that are stronger than any foe known to the church.

Such principles will enable Christians like you and me to stand in the storm. They will give the true follower of Christ the strength to endure the brisk gales of persecution and emerge even stronger.

Here are two basic principles from the suffering church that can lead us into victory as we see the gathering storm. First, believe in the Bible as God's inspired, inerrant Word. Second, commit to obey fully the principles and teachings found in the Bible. It's in these two basic principles that Christians throughout the centuries have found a firm foundation. The Bible has been an oasis in the deserts of life. It's the foundation-rock upon which Jesus said we should build our lives.

When he arrived at the border, the guards began immediately searching his vehicle for Bibles. He told me later, " . . . I now understand that there is a great spiritual battle taking place at that border. Satan doesn't want the Bible in the hands of our people."

One of my great concerns today about our ability to withstand the storm is that the church is quickly becoming biblically illiterate. Doctrine is out and experience is in. Unity of spirit has replaced integrity of belief. Need-centered preaching has taken precedent over biblical exposition. Without a clear knowledge and acceptance of Scripture as inerrant and practical for Christian living, we cannot confront falsehood and stand in the midst of persecution. In fact, cults are expanding at a rapid rate and converting many church members who don't have a biblical foundation for their lives.

A few years ago I addressed a group of Southern Baptist evangelism leaders at a national conference in Salt Lake City, the home of Mormonism. While there, several of us took a tour of some of the historical sites of the Mormon church. A young woman from Houston led our tour and told us that she had been a member of a well-known Southern Baptist congregation in Houston before she converted to Mormonism. From what I've seen, her story isn't all that unusual. The two most predominant offshoots of Christianity in America are Mormonism and Jehovah's Witnesses. Much of their growth in America and around the world has come from biblically illiterate church members. And since the collapse of the Soviet Union both groups have flooded into Eastern Europe.

THE BIBLE'S POWER

The Bible has given Christians the power to withstand intimidation and persecution. Before the collapse of the Iron Curtain, the greatest fear of the communists was the Bible. During the reign of the communists in the former Soviet Union, I talked to a young communist in Kishinev, the capital of Moldova. At that time the Bible was a forbidden book in this young man's country. As we discussed my faith in Christ and his atheism, he hesitated for a moment and then said, "I guess you have a point. If the Bible is not true, then why do we fear it so much?"

One of the greatest concerns among the communists was the Christian's possession of the Bible. Once a pastor friend of mine from Romania had the opportunity to visit the West during the Ceaucescu regime. When he drove back to Romania, he saw for the first time what many of us had seen for years. When he arrived at the border, the guards began immediately searching his vehicle for Bibles. He told me later, "Sammy, I never understood what you went through when you came to our country. But I now understand that there is a great spiritual battle taking place at that border. Satan doesn't want the Bible in the hands of our people."

My friend was right. But after freedom came to Eastern Europe, I spoke in a remote region of Siberia, where no churches had existed. Many people came to know Christ through our meetings and a church was born. During our follow-up sessions the new converts could ask anything they wish about God, the Bible, and their new life in Christ. The first questions were about the cults. Many had already made their way to this remote region of Siberia. One of the things that I said to those new believers was that "the Bible was the greatest threat to the kingdom of darkness before the communists fell.

"Now that freedom has come to the Soviet Union, the Bible is still the greatest threat to the kingdom of darkness," I explained. "There will be groups who will come here and try to replace the Scriptures as your sole source of authority and belief. They will normally attempt to make one of the following the final source of authority for your life: (1) tradition, (2) experience, (3) another religious book, or (4) a human personality. However," I said, "stick with the Bible. Satan tried to keep it out of your hands when the communists ruled. The communists are no longer here, but Satan is. He will try to replace the Bible with a source of authority that's completely inadequate. The church survived under repression because it held tightly to the Bible as the Word of God. It will survive in freedom only because it holds tightly to the Word of God."

Christians in the East survived a very dark night because they believed the Scriptures to be the infallible Word of God. They hungered for the Bible. They read the Bible, studied it, memorized it, and lived by it no matter what it cost them. We in the West must have the same hunger for God's Word if we are to stand in the storm. As those who know and love God's Word, we will become beacons, not flickering in fear but shining in hope.

Once in Romania, a group of young Romanian singers accompanied me as I preached throughout the nation. This had never been done before. It could have been very dangerous for those young people. They could have lost their educational opportunities. But they were willing to sacrifice their futures to proclaim the Bible as God's Word.

In order to be in this youth singing group, a person had to not only be willing to lay his life and future on the line, but he had to memorize the books of James, 1 John, and 1 Peter. When the group sang before I preached, they would quote a chapter of one of those books of the Bible and then sing a song. Before they sang another song they quoted another chapter. It was magnificent to listen to those young people. But I've often wondered how many singing groups we would have in America if a requirement to be in the singing group would be to memorize three books of the Bible. I'm afraid there wouldn't be too many.

But it was more than simply a revering the Scriptures that enabled the church in Eastern Europe to survive a dark night. It was also a deep commitment to obey the Bible. Many in the West would heartily agree, saying, "I believe the Bible to be true and accurate. It's the Word of God." However, I'm afraid their commitment to study the Scriptures would be very weak. And their commitment to obey the Bible would be even weaker.

Jesus made some very important remarks concerning obedience to His Word. He said, "Whoever has my commands and obeys them, he is the one who loves me. He who loves me will be loved by my Father, and I too will love him and show myself to him" (John 14:21). Many in the Western world who have the Word of God in their possession would say, "I love Jesus." But the true test of our love for Jesus is whether we will obey His Word. We can say all day long that we love God, but we're just filling the air with religious talk unless we are willing to obey what He has said.

But there was a second thing that Jesus said about obedience to His Word. He said, "Therefore everyone who hears these words of mine and puts them into practice is like a wise man who built his house on the rock" (Matthew 7:24). When the storms of life come, obedience to the Word of God builds a foundation in our lives that enables us to stand securely in the storm. A lack of obedience produces just the opposite. Jesus said, "But everyone who hears these words of mine and does not put them into practice is like a foolish man who built his house on sand. The rain came down, the streams rose, and the winds blew and beat against that house, and it fell with a great crash" (Matthew 7:26, 27).

Perhaps that's the major reason that in a nation such as America, which professes a belief in the Bible, many Christians seem to be drowning in the storms of life. We say we believe in the Scriptures, but refuse to place our lives under the Bible's authority. The return of Christ appears to be imminent. The storm clouds are beginning to gather. The world stands on the brink of some of the greatest times of darkness in its history. The question that continues to haunt me at the close of this century and millennium is simply that of the chancellor of the National University of Rwanda, "Where is the church?"

Where will the church stand in these days of momentous change? Will it stand on the shifting sands of pluralism, or will it stand on the sure foundation of the Word of God? Will it adopt a philosophy of cultural Christianity or will it become a lighthouse on the solid rock of biblical Christianity?

Darkness approaches. The winds have begun to blow. The rain is coming. But a beacon continues to shine. If you desire to be a beam in that shining beacon, believe the central message of the Bible—the good news of Christ's sacrifice and His words of love. Believe in Him. Follow Him. Obey Him. When the storms of life come, you will stand. When the winds of adversity blow, you will overcome. When the torrential rains of the world fall, you will have a secure shelter. When the floodwaters rise, they will not overcome you. Christ will be the rock of your salvation. And, standing on that rock, you can become part of the beacon shining through the storm.

NOTES

Introduction: The Coming Fire

1. See Matthew 16:27; John 14:2-3; and Acts 1:11.
2. American Airlines brochure, American Airlines Admirals Club, O'Hare Airport, Chicago.
3. "North Atlantic Air Traffic Forecasts for the Years 1993–98, 2000, 2005, 2010," Report of Congressional Information Services, Inc. (Washington, D.C., 1993).
4. Jonathan Mann as quoted in Laurie Garrett, *The Coming Plague* (New York: Farrar, Straus and Giroux, 1994), xii. Garrett, a health and science journalist, notes that "In that scenario [with 110 million infected], 25 million would have died of AIDS between 1980 and 2000."
5. Garrett, *The Coming Plague*, 486.
6. Ibid, xii.
7. Yonah Alexander, ed., rev. ed., *International Terrorism* (New York: Praeger, 1976), xvii.
8. Eric Morris and Alan Hoe, *Terrorism: Threat and Response* (London: McMillan, 1987) 19, 16.
9. Vic Sussman, "Hate, Murder, and Mayhem on the Net," *U.S. News and World Report*, 22 May 1995, 62.
10. "Teens' Time Bomb Foiled," Associated Press, 2 February 1996, Internet file V0637, 01:21 EST.
11. Steven Levy, "Techno Mania," *Newsweek*, 27 February 1995, 26.

12. One eighteen-month study directed by Martin Rimm of Carnegie-Mellon University found on-line pornography to be pervasive. According to an Associated Press report, "The study found pornography is one of the largest, if not the largest recreational uses of computer networks. Nearly all the users are men. Half the 8.5 million images called up in the last five years from commercial adult bulletin boards nationwide depicted pedophilia, bestiality, bondage, sado-masochism, transsexualism and sex involving urination or defecation. . . . The World Wide Web is making access to many of these images as easy as a few clicks of a button." Associated Press Release, June 28, 1995, Internet file VO315, 06:47 EDT.

13. Anthony Spaeth, "Engineer of Doom," *Time*, 12 June 1995, 57.

14. Ibid.

Chapter 1: The Rise of the Lawless Spirit

1. Tom Masland, "The Return of Terror," *Newsweek*, 8 August 1994, 24.

2. "America's Globo-Cop," *Newsweek*, 16 October 1995, 52.

3. Dorinda Elliot and Melinda Liu, "Hostile Takeover," *Newsweek*, 2 October 1995, 10.

4. Jonathan Beaty, "Russia's Yard Sale," *Time*, 18 April 1994, 52.

5. Bruce Nelan, "Hitting Back at Terrorists," *Time*, 5 July 1993, 28.

6. Ibid.

7. Craig Whitney, "Plutonium for Sale. Call 1-800-TERROR," *New York Times*, 21 August 1994, "The Week in Review," 1.

8. Bruce Nelan, "Formula for Terror," *Time*, 29 August 1994, 47.

9. Patrick Theros, "Current Trends in Global Terrorism," U.S. Department of State Dispatch, 5, no. 25 (20 June 1994): 415.

10. Robert Landon, "Putting a Stop to Narco-Terrorism," *Police Chief,* June 1987, 9.

11. Bruce Nelan, "Hitting Back at Terrorists," 28.

12. Mary Ellen Sullivan, "Drugs, the World Picture," *Current Health* 16 (2 February 1990): 4.

13. Michael Specter, "New Moscow Mob Terror," *New York Times,* 10 June 1994.

14. Brian Crozier, "The New World Disorder," *National Review,* 19 December 1994, 49.

15. Tom Masland, "The Return of Terror," 24.

16. "Suicide Bus Bombings Against Israel" (chart), *San Antonio Express-News,* 22 August 1995, 7A.

17. *Vine's Expository Dictionary of New Testament Words,* (Nashville: Nelson, 1985).

18. Ibid.

Chapter 2: False Messiahs and False Prophets

1. Ian Buruma, "Lost Without a Faith," *Time,* 3 April 1995, 34.

2. Elizabeth Gleick, "The Strangers Among Us," *People,* 19 April 1993, 34.

3. Bruce W. Nelan, "The Price of Fanaticism," *Time,* 3 April 1995, 38.

4. Ibid., 39.

5. Richard Lacayo, "In the Name of God," *Time,* 15 March 1993, 36.

6. Ibid.

7. Ibid.

8. Malcolm Gray, "Kiev's Cult of Doom," *Maclean's,* 22 November 1993, 32.

9. Ibid.

10. Richard Lacayo, "In the Reign of Fire," *Time,* 17 October 1994, 59.

11. Ibid.

12. Alan Cooperman, "The Same Couldn't Happen Here." *U.S. News and World Report,* 3 April 1995, 36.
13. Richard Jerome, "Japan's Mad Messiah," *People Weekly,* 12 June 1995, 48.
14. Ibid.
15. David VanBrena, "Prophet of Poison," *Time,* 3 April 1995, 29.
16. Ibid., 28–29.

Chapter 3: Wars and Rumors of Wars

1. Ruben Mendez, "Paying for Peace and Development," *Foreign Policy,* 100 (Fall 1995): 21.
2. "Chronicles," *Time,* 2 May 1994, 13.
3. Mendez, "Paying for Peace and Development," 21.
4. Austin Bay, "Wider Balkan War Probable," *San Antonio Express-News,* 31 August 1995, 4B.
5. Ray Marshall, "The Global Jobs Crisis," Charles Maynes, ed., *Foreign Policy* (New York: Carnegie, 1995), 50.
6. "Defectors Reveal Files on Biological Weapons Agenda," *San Antonio Express-News,* 22 August 1995, 7A.
7. "U.N. Envoy Says Iraqi Germ Warfare Agents Could Kill Everyone" *San Antonio Express-News,* 4 August 1995, 12A.
8. Christopher Dickey, "Plagues in the Making," *Newsweek,* 9 October 1995, 50.
9. Ibid.
10. See "Iraq Link to Poison Chemicals Revealed," *San Antonio Express-News,* 3 September 1995, 23A. The article from the Associated Press cites "documents obtained by *U.S. News and World Report* [saying] traces of chemicals were found on the battlefield."
11. Yossef Bodansky, *Crisis in Korea* (New York: SPI Books, 1994), 272.
12. Ibid., 233, 234.

13. Douglas Waller, "Onward Cyber Soldiers," *Time,* 21 August 1995, 39–40.

14. Ruben Mendez, "Paying for Peace and Development," 22.

15. Ibid.

Chapter 4: Globalization of Infectious Diseases

1. Richard Preston, *The Hot Zone* (New York: Random House, 1994), 16–17.

2. Ibid., 12.

3. Associated Press, 18 May 1995, Compuserve file 17:04 EDT, V0387.

4. Associated Press, 18 May 1995, Compuserve file 21:52 EDT, V0590.

5. *Economist,* 20 May 1995, 79.

6. Laurie Garrett, *The Coming Plague* (New York: Farrar, Straus and Giroux, 1994), 53, 54.

7. Preston, *The Hot Zone,* 68.

8. "Why Viruses Push Our Hot Button," *Newsweek,* 22 May 1995, 54.

9. One researcher at the Centers for Disease Control in Atlanta said, "I can't put my finger on why Reston doesn't make us sick. Personally, I wouldn't feel comfortable handling it without a suit and maximum containment procedures." See Preston, *The Hot Zone,* 260.

10. Shannon Brownlee, "The Disease Busters," *U.S. News and World Report,* 27 March 1995, 50.

11. Ibid., 52.

12. Anita Manning, "Scientists Say New Virus Could Cause Pandemic," *USA Today,* 17 January 1996, 1A.

13. Stephen Morse, "Factors in the Emergence of Infectious Diseases," *Perspectives* 1, no.1 (January–March 1995).

14. "The Threat of Infectious Diseases in Somalia," *New England Journal of Medicine* 328, no.14 (8 April 1993): 1061.

Chapter 5: Globalization of HIV

1. Robert Swenson, "Plagues, History, and AIDS," *American Scholar*, Spring 1988, 191, 192.
2. Laurie Garrett, *The Coming Plague* (New York: Farrar, Straus and Giroux, 1994), 362.
3. Ibid.
4. Phyllida Brown, "Controversy over Origin of AIDS," *New Scientist*, 30 November 1991, 22.
5. Wayne Biddle, *Field Guide to Germs* (New York: Henry Holt, 1995), 78.
6. John Lagone, *AIDS, the Facts* (New York: Little, Brown, 1991), 14–15.
7. World Health Organization Report, vol. 21, no. 1 (Geneve, Switzerland: WHO, 1968), 24.
8. As cited in "Aids Brief," *MAP International Newsletter*, First Quarter 1995, 1.
9. Jonathan Mann, "The International Epidemiology of AIDS," *Scientific American*, October 1988, 82.
10. Lawrence Altman, "Earliest AIDS Case Is Called into Doubt," *New York Times*, 4 April 1995, C3.
11. As cited in "Aids Brief," *MAP International Newsletter*, 1.
12. Phyllida Brown, "Sex and Drugs Spread Different Types of HIV," *New Scientist*, 25 July 1992, 6.
13. Lawrence Altman, *"Earliest AIDS Case,"* C3.
14. William E. Paul, "Reexamining AIDS Research Priorities," *Science*, 3 February 1995, 633.
15. Tara Patel, "France's AIDS Time Bomb," *New Scientist*, 13 August 1994, 13.
16. Phyllida Brown, "Will the Strain Show in Bangkok," *New Scientist*, 7 January 1995, 12.
17. Bob Drogin, "S. Africa Takes First Steps to Fight Rising AIDS Rate," *Los Angeles Times*, 22 July 1995, A2.
18. *New Scientist*, January 7, 1995, 12.
19. Garrett, *The Coming Plague*, 389.

20. Ibid., 386.
21. "Diseases of the Bible," in *Nelson's Illustrated Bible Dictionary*, Herbert Locckyer, Sr., ed. (Nashville: Nelson, 1986).
22. *Vine's Expository Dictionary of New Testament Words*, s.v. "pestilence" (Nashville: Nelson, 1985).

Chapter 6: Natural Disasters

1. Anne-Christine d'Adesky, "Preparing the World for Disaster," *UN Chronicle* 28 (June 1991): 40.
2. Jack Williams, *USA Today Weather Almanac 1995* (New York: Vintage, 1994), 5.
3. Ibid., 1.
4. "Reading the Patterns," *Economist*, 1 April 1995, 65.
5. "Storm Surge," *San Antonio Express-News*, 12 November 1995, 12A.
6. Douglas Cogan, *The Greenhouse Gambit*, A 1992 report by Investor Responsibility Research Center, 1755 Massachusetts Ave., Washington, D.C., p. v.
7. "Theory of Global Warming Supported by Climate Studies," *Chicago Tribune*, 4 January 1996, 1:3.
8. Ibid.
9. "The Air: Hot Times All Around," *Time* (International Edition), 30 October 1995, 65.
10. "The Land: Less Milk and Honey," *Time* (International Edition), 30 October 1995, 52.
11. *USA Today Weather Almanac*, 14.
12. Ibid.
13. Bruce Bolts, *Earthquakes* (New York: W. H. Freeman and Company, 1993), 98.
14. Bob Holmes, "Big One Threatens the Big Apple," *New Scientist*, 4 March 1995, 11.
15. Bernice Wuethr, "It's Official: Quake Danger in Northwest Rivals California's," *Science*, 23 September 1994, 1802.

16. Bob Holmes, "Big Crunch Looms for Northern India," *New Scientist*, 17 December 1994, 6.

17. Richard Kerr, "Bigger Jolts Are on the Way for Southern California," *Science*, 13 January 1995, 176.

18. James Cox, "Quake Could Rock World Economy," *USA Today*, 20 January 1995, 1B.

19. Ibid.

20. "Will the World Starve?" *Economist*, 10 June 1995, 40.

21. "The Land: Less Milk and Honey" *Time*, 30 October 1995, 53.

22. Sandra Postel, "Water Scarcity," *Environmental Science and Technology*, 26, no.2 (December 1992): 2332.

23. "Ending Deaths from Famine," *New England Journal of Medicine* 328 (8 April 1993): 1056.

24. David Perlman, "Scientists Warn of Asteroids," *San Francisco Chronicle*, 23 May 1995, A1.

25. Ibid.

Chapter 7: Fulfilling the Great Commission
1. *Matthew Henry's Commentary on the Whole Bible*, vol. 3 (Grand Rapids: Guardian Press, 1976), 202.

2. "Christians Mobilized for Evangelism," *Center Line* (a publication of the Billy Graham Center at Wheaton Illinois College), Summer 1995.

3. *Astra Marketing Report*, Half-year 1994, n.p.

Chapter 8: The Great Persecution
1. Kim A. Lawton, "Killed in the Line of Duty," *Charisma*, October 1995, 59.

2. *Koha Jone*, 25 September 1995, 1.

3. Mary Ann Tucker and Sharon Young, "Why Are People Heterosexuals?" Handout 12, CCS Diversity Workshop, Indianapolis, 1995. Sponsored by AT&T.

4. "Florida Baptists Boycott Disney over Slide," *Tampa Tribune*, 16 November 1995, 1:1, 13

5. John Walvoord, *The Revelation of Jesus Christ* (Chicago: Moody, 1966), 124.

6. David Barrett and Frank Jansen, *Congress Notebook* (Manila: Lausanne II Congress on World Evangelization), sec. 13:13.

7. Lawton, "Killed in the Line of Duty," 56.

Chapter 9: The Only Safe Place

1. G. Campbell Morgan, *The Bible and the Cross* (Grand Rapids: Baker, 1975), 126, 128.

2. If you have prayed for God to forgive your sins and Jesus to become part of your life, please write to Moody Press for information to help you grow in your faith. Write to the address on the final page of this book. And write to me in care of Moody Press, so I can rejoice with you and pray for your spiritual walk with God. Welcome to the family of God!

Chapter 10: The Transformed Christian

1. F. F. Bruce, *The Spreading Flame*, (Grand Rapids: Eerdmans, 1979), 177.

Chapter 11: Compassionate Evangelism

1. F. F. Bruce, *The Spreading Flame*, (Grand Rapids: Eerdmans, 1979), 177.

2. "Step by Step," *Challenge*, November/December 1995, 33.

3. Ibid.

4. Ibid., 36.

5. Telephone interview with Erwin McManus, 6 January 1996.

Chapter 12: Standing in the Storm

1. R. C. Sproul, *Essential Truths of the Christian Faith* (Wheaton, Ill.: Tyndale, 1992), 16.

Moody Press, a ministry of Moody Bible Institute,
is designed for education, evangelization, and edification
If we may assist you in knowing more about Christ
and the Christian life, please write us without obligation:
Moody Press, c/o MLM, Chicago, Illinois 60610.